Learning

'Twin foci characterize this enjoyable book: a raw reality that reflects the everyday experience of a Christian who is not a religious professional and the choices we all have to make, and a refusal to compromise the priority of Christ in our lives. Full of spiritual wisdom, Neil's writing is marked by a rare honesty. It made me think time and time again. It should guide many struggling with difficult life choices and help keep their priorities clear.'
Dr Derek Tidball, Principal, London School of Theology

'I have enjoyed reading it immensely – I couldn't put it down! I think this is the most challenging, relevant, straightforward book I have read on contemporary discipleship . . . a "must read."'
Jill Garrett, Caret

'This is vintage stuff from a writer whose ratings increase as a foremost Christian author with every fresh volume . . . In the final, moving chapter Neil bravely lifts the curtain – we view his personal struggle as once more he battles with cancer . . . I predict this book will be *the* spiritual manual for Christians in the 21st century as we endeavour to live out our faith in the complexities of so called post-modernity where all is flux and nothing is certain. Thanks Prof – we are grateful!'
Tony Sargent, International Christian College

'Looking for an MOT test for your life? Neil Hood provides us all with incisive, vital questions. And he writes from the Crossroads himself. Tender, authentic, and laced with grace.'
Jeff Lucas, author, speaker, broadcaster

'Balanced, practical and inspiring . . . full of spiritual common sense.'
Adrian Plass

'Read this book! Neil Hood knows his Lord and writes with penetrating insight, born out of his own experience, into the subtle ways in which all of us can be led astray. His passion to communicate what he has learned from God has carried him through the very difficult circumstances, explained inside, under which this book was written.'
Annabel Robinson, Professor of Classics, University of Regina, Canada

Learning at the Crossroads
A Traveller's Guide to Christian Life

Neil Hood

Authentic

Contents

Dedication

To the glory of God and the building up of his people on earth; and in profound gratitude to the global army of prayer warriors who have sustained Anna and me and our family (Annette, Alan and Emily; Cameron, Ann, Isla and Sarah) during my current serious illness. Without you this book would never have been written.

Preface

Have you ever been on a long and complex journey without any clues about the way ahead? Welcome to the journey of life! All of us need guidance on this journey – even though we may not always know this and even though we don't always look for guidance from the right sources. In principle, Christians should adopt these words from Thomas à Kempis, "They travel lightly whom God's grace carries". But sometimes the travelling feels more exacting than that. And while all of us need guidance every day, we are sometimes only conscious of this need when it becomes pressing, in what I call "crossroads" situations. For most of us, life is full of such crossroads. They are often times of disruption, indecision, conflicting choices and uncertainty – but, when the issues are resolved in the way that the Lord intended, they can also be times of blessing and recovery. We can encounter crossroads in our careers, friendships, relationships, church, work, service, geographical location and so on.

This book explores a number of lessons that I have learned at several different types of crossroads. I always find it encouraging to learn that many great biblical characters have had similar experiences. I wish I had been able to read a book like this when I was starting out on my own Christian life, before I reached some of my own critical crossroads experiences. My purpose in writing, therefore, is to encourage other Christians travelling on the same journey. In sharing some of these experiences and hard-learned lessons I do not seek to idealize or glorify my personal behaviour – quite the contrary! I have made many mistakes along the road, I have been slow to learn from different experiences, and I have not always seen the Lord's will quickly enough. It is, in effect, a traveller's guide. Many of us buy travel guides but don't use them, while others of us read them and argue with the advice they offer. Still more of us, however, never even buy the travel guide or map – we avoid asking anyone for directions, preferring to struggle on unaided. Our pride and misplaced self-confidence set us on an autopilot course. In order to steer Christians back onto the right course, this book explores fundamental principles that govern many crossroads decisions – principles that Christians ignore at their peril.

It may help you to know a little about the context in which this book was written. Out of years of experience and months of prayer, this book began to take shape in January 2004 – only a few weeks before I was faced with a serious personal crossroads concerning my health. I have shared more about this particular crossroads in Chapter 11. Although the Lord has used my personal circumstances to help me focus my thoughts on the subject, the issues covered in this book are crucial for all of Christian life – not just for specific trials and crises.

There are many different factors that influence which path we take in life. Nature and nurture, education and training, personalities and advisers, crises and opportunities, friends and peers are only a few of them. Sometimes these factors appear to operate in random ways – making it seem as though chance plays a role in the outcomes of our lives. But chance is not a concept that sits comfortably with Christians – nor should it. However, in the confusion of life at the crossroads, Christians are sometimes tempted to look for signs and signals from all kinds of unwholesome sources. Because we are often vulnerable when we reach such crossroads, even Christians entertain suggestions from sources that they would do well to ignore. The Bible is full of relevant advice for all the situations we face in life, and this book seeks to help Christians both find and apply its advice to crossroads situations.

Before you start reading, it might help you to recall what your major crossroad experiences have been. This book is not only for the hesitant or indecisive. It's amazing how many strong people feel weak when faced with big decisions. So it is with the mature and immature, the pastor and the lay member, the leader and the follower – all of us, whoever we are, need advice sometimes. Crossroads experiences confront all of us: anyone making a career choice, including a career switch; people selecting a partner for life; the young married couple deciding on lifestyle balance; the mature person facing unemployment; someone confronted by a health and family crisis; those contemplating the use of their time in retirement; and, indeed, all of us who make big decisions in the course of ordinary everyday life. There are crossroads everywhere. While this book cannot cover all of life's experiences in detail, the principles here can be applied to a wide variety of situations. My aim is twofold: first, to help you think about the consequences of past crossroads decisions and second, to better equip you for the crossroads today and tomorrow.

Style and content. The roots of this book are firmly planted in the soil of the Bible. Its principles are on every page, and every element – including case studies, stories, personal experiences, characterizations of behaviour, tabulations and so on – is designed to reinforce biblical principles. The book is interactive – that is, there are lots of opportunities for you to think about your own life and apply these principles, engaging you in the content. Each chapter stands on its own, so you don't need to follow them in sequence and you can dip into any chapter to take one of the sub-sections away for careful thought. I regularly refer to other Christian writers, and in many instances I illustrate principles by quotations from standard sources.'[1]

Structure. The book has ten chapters and an epilogue. The title of each chapter is a clear instruction, and the chapter itself explores the principles behind it in a variety of ways. I am comfortable with setting these out as instructions, because they reflect some of the clear biblical mandates that God gives us. Each chapter is designed to catch your attention, engage your mind and inform your response. It's then that the Spirit of the Lord takes over. The book demands a response from its readers, and I make no apology for that. These ten main lessons comprise the list of milestones at which I have had to regularly pause throughout the busyness of my life – and still do. While not every decision is a crossroads, and not every crossroads is a crisis, some are both.

Acknowledgements. This is my fourth Christian book, and the list of those deserving acknowledgement grows ever longer. The feedback from the readers of the *Whose Life* trilogy has continued to be a great encouragement and blessing to me. Five years ago I wondered whether I should write Christian books. Now I know that I should. But this particular volume is unique in that only by the power of the persistent prayers of countless people across the world have I been able to write it. I also acknowledge the many people who have helped me at times of crossroads, and the others whose experiences have informed me for good or ill on the themes contained in this book. Once again I also thank those who have kindly endorsed the book. Their contribution is invaluable in positioning it among the diverse readership community. On the publishing and production side, the team remains the same and their contribution is as vital as ever. Irene Hood, my personal assistant, remains a tower of strength for her support, organizational skills and attention to detail. Mark Finnie and the Authentic team continue to be a great source of guidance and encouragement; and my editor Tara Smith is as clear-thinking and thought-stimulating as ever.

Neil Hood
December 2004

---

[1]   These quotations come from a wide range of Christian websites and published sources. The latter include: John Blanchard, *Gathered Gold* (Darlington: Evangelical Press, 1984) and *Sifted Silver* (Darlington: Evangelical Press, 1984); Edythe Draper, *Quotations for the Christian World* (Wheaton, IL: Tyndale, 1992); F.B. Proctor, *Treasury of Quotations on Religious Subjects* (Grand Rapids: Kregel Publications, 1977); Robert Backhouse, *5,000 Quotations for Teachers and Preachers* (Eastbourne: Kingsway Publications, 1994); *The Times Book of Quotations* (London: HarperCollins, 2000).

Biographical Note

Neil Hood, CBE, DBA, FRSE, juggles a busy life as an international business strategist, university professor, company director, Christian conference speaker, prolific author on international business and economic development, family man and church elder. He is Emeritus Professor of Business Policy at the University of Strathclyde, Glasgow, UK and a director of, or adviser to, a number of major companies including Scottish Power plc, Xansa plc and Reg Vardy plc. He has advised many governments and international agencies on economic matters. He is Chairman of Scottish Equity Partners Ltd., and of the Clyde Waterfront Strategic Partnership Board. In 2000 he was honoured by Queen Elizabeth for services to business and economic development. His life-plan to dedicate his time and skills to Christian ministries is reflected in his chairmanship of Send the Light Ltd., in his involvement with Christian ministries such as Blythswood Care and International Christian College, and in his busy preaching and teaching schedule. He and his wife, Anna, have two children, Annette (married to Alan) and Cameron (married to Ann), and three grandchildren, Emily, Isla and Sarah. Neil is not too busy, however, to grow orchids, cheer on the Scottish rugby team, play with his grandchildren . . . or pray that *Learning at the Crossroads* will help you see past decision points in context and prepare you for current and future ones.

1

Never Trust a Prince

"It is better to take refuge in the LORD than to trust in man. It is better to take refuge in the LORD than to trust in princes." (Ps.118:8,9)

Outline

In laying the foundations and establishing a framework for the book, this chapter looks at the following issues:

Learning at the crossroads: What does it mean to learn at the crossroads?

Why you should never trust a prince: Why is it dangerous to trust princes?

Looking back: A few lessons from the crossroads: What can such experiences teach us about princes, crossroads, ourselves and God?

Back to basics: How can we distinguish between different types of trust?

Case study: Nehemiah and the princes: What did Nehemiah learn at the crossroads?

Learning at the crossroads

Maps, if we use them correctly, can give us fascinating clues to culture and history and can help us get where we want to go. We can travel to very few destinations without coming to an intersection, where we face choices and some degree of uncertainty. Some will pause and consult a map; others will take longer to thoroughly appraise the options; while still others will barrel through with little consideration. Some will see the possibilities offered by different alternatives, while others will see danger at the crossroads. As with any journey, we will inevitably come to crossroads in life as well. At these points, we need to make choices about which path to take. As we shall explore throughout this book, these crossroads experiences are times of opportunity and learning.

The Christian encounters many different types of crossroads. Sometimes we only realize the significance of a particular crossroads decision in retrospect, but at other times we are deeply conscious of the consequences of taking a certain direction and realize that it will be life changing. Charles Swindoll says that "The process involved in redirecting our lives is often painful, slow and even confusing. Occasionally it seems unbearable." By definition, the Christian travels through life with a map. But travelling with a map and consulting one are two quite different things. I have many maps in my car but rarely use any of them. Why? Most of the routes I take are familiar ones, and consulting a map is simply not necessary. I do need a map when the route is unfamiliar, or complex, or when I haven't driven somewhere in a long time. Lots of people – including many Christians – use the Bible that way – as a "crisis manual" to be dusted off at life's crossroads experiences. In this book I want to encourage you to engage with the Bible in a different way. In the Bible God gives us a rich resource of wisdom and guidance for all of life's challenges, as well as many accounts of people who faced physical, personal and spiritual crossroads. We will learn from these people and their experiences throughout this book.

While crossroads experiences are all different, for the Christian the most important is our decision to accept Jesus Christ as Saviour and Lord. Other major crossroads experiences involve relationships, family, career, location, friendships, church and so on. On a daily basis, too, we are challenged about our relationship with the Lord – and called to a quality of obedience that we are inclined to resist. What do we need to make good and godly decisions when we come to these crossroads?

Perspective: We need spiritual guidance to know the relative importance of the decisions we are making. Every crossroads is not a crisis. And some crossroads become crises only because of our perspective, or lack thereof. Sometimes we ask for God's guidance but don't really want it or seek to follow it – which is a form of hypocrisy. As C.S. Lewis wisely wrote, "A glimpse of the next three feet of road is more important and useful than a view of the horizon".

Time: Sometimes we need to spend more time at the crossroads than we do. Time is often at a premium and, not wanting to appear indecisive, we feel under pressure to make up our minds. On the other hand, there are some who camp at crossroads for years – immobilized by fear, uncertainty and even an unwillingness to take a risk for God. God's timing, of course, cannot be discerned by our calendar or wrist-watch.

Support: I have seen many Christians standing at a crossroads alone, without the benefit of help from others they can trust. Some of us are better at consulting other people, while others are fearful of revealing their dilemmas or disclosing their frailties. I confess that I have not often shared my own crossroads experiences while they were happening – I preferred to resolve them myself, but at a cost to my peace of mind. I have been privileged to help others in similar situations, however, and have seen how the support of another person can be particularly beneficial in terms of putting decisions in context.

Willingness to learn: Crossroads experiences shape our lives. Learning from the process of decision-making helps us to grow in our Christian faith and also enables us to help others travelling the same road. If you have never done it before, try writing down what you have learned from your past crossroads experiences – and then look out for someone you could help. There are plenty of people facing these decisions all around you, but you might need to take the initiative to offer to help.

REFLECTION:

Have you had the appropriate perspective, time and support when you have reached different crossroads? What have you learned from these experiences? Reflect in particular on God's timing for these crossroads and praise him for his wisdom – as you pray for your own patience.

Why you should never trust a prince

The verses from Psalm 118 above are important for every Christian – regardless of era, culture or context. Psalm 118:8 is reported to be the central verse of the Bible – but it is also the central voice of the Bible. In Jesus' own words, ". . . and the sheep listen to his voice. He calls his own sheep by name and leads them out".[1] All disciples need to learn the tone, timbre and force of that voice; we all need to be able to recognize it amidst the noise of life. This particular instruction regarding trust lies at the centre of our Christian faith, and we must continuously heed it throughout our lives. In the words of Simon Peter, "You alone have the words that give eternal life."[2] If only we truly believed that!

All of us place some degree of trust in "princes" – those who exercise some sort of power over us in work, social, political or family life – of one kind or another. Since society can only function on a basis of trust, we quite rightly think of most of these relationships as being unremarkable. "After all, I have to trust my boss to be reasonable in how he looks after my interests – unless I have evidence to the contrary." "When I pay my tax bill, I trust the government in power to use that money wisely for the common good of the country." "When the police redirected me to take an hour-long detour, I had to trust them without knowing what had happened on the usual route – I know they don't close major roads for no reason." These situations are all part of everyday life. The verse in Psalm 118, however, refers to a far more fundamental degree of trust. In whom do we place our faith and confidence? Upon whom are we dependent? To whom do we give our allegiance? And, ultimately, who is the master of our lives?

Looking back:
A few lessons from the crossroads

I have felt the power of princes most acutely at crossroads experiences involving my career. While academia has always been at the core of my professional life, I have also had extensive involvement in business and public life. I have been fortunate to have had a variety of desirable and rather radical career choices. And, at these crossroads, various "princes" have tried to exercise influence over my choice of direction in order to further their own ends. I have often found it difficult to see clearly what God wanted me to do. It has been far from easy, and I have not always worked it out perfectly. I have spent months at a time at crossroads, trying to resolve all of the issues involved. Following are three of my career crossroads experiences.

A prince with money: When I was in my twenties, I was involved in researching and advising in the textile industry. In response to several provocative articles I had written for business magazines about the future of this industry, one of the leading entrepreneurs in the industry contacted me. He was the head of a large and highly acquisitive public company with global interests. He and his advisers were at odds over how to rationalize this multi-branded group after a spate of acquisitions – and these were the issues about which I was writing. He and I happened to be on the same wavelength about the future of his business. I admired this man immensely. He was intelligent, energetic, innovative and highly personable. He was also very demanding and ruthless in his treatment of his senior people. They rapidly moved from "favoured son" to "readily dispensable" status if they let him down in any way. I worked closely with him as his strategy adviser for over three years and enjoyed it very much. Towards the end of these three years, when I was thirty years old, he pounced with an attractive offer and a large pay cheque. "The logic of moving ahead with the diversification project that you have been working on with me is that you join us as its managing director. Whatever your academic salary is, I will multiply it by three." I had arrived at the crossroads – but it was one that I had seen coming. He had been hinting for a long time that it was a waste that I was still in academic life, and he had told me that I could have a very bright future in business. I confess that it was not a profound sense of holiness that made me reject this offer. His wealth and the stress that he placed on money were alien to me, and he had misjudged me in thinking that this would sway me. As a married man with two children and a mortgage I can't say that I wasn't tempted. But, admire and respect him though I did for his abilities and achievements, I knew that his values and mine were very different and I did not want to put my life in his hands. Most critically, I was convinced that this was not where God wanted me to be. To work for this particular taskmaster would be all-consuming and incompatible with other objectives that the Lord had set in my heart. I did not stay at this particular crossroads for long. My colleague was shocked that I rejected his offer, and our relationship was never the same after that. My explanation cut no ice with him, and I did not expect it to – I was serving another master he neither knew nor understood.

Princes with praise: On several occasions I have experienced the seductive power of praise, flattery and various forms of acclaim. Most of us are vulnerable in this area, and we will consider it in more detail in Chapter 5. It is delightful to be recognized and encouraged, even if we respond with protestations of humility. But others can use praise as a form of power to achieve the ends they desire. One example from my experience illustrates this point well. When I was fifty years old, recruitment consultants approached me to take up the post of vice-chancellor of a university. Although I was flattered, I had not seen this as the way ahead for me. Out of courtesy, however, I agreed to meet the consultant. I also wanted to make sure that, if this was a crossroads, I had at least looked carefully at the route ahead. After this meeting, two or three senior people from the university concerned requested a meeting with me. My inclination was not to take the matter further – but I was pressed hard to at least allow the university to make its case directly to me. When I arrived for this meeting, in a hotel, I was confronted by a group of 12 people – among whom were some powerful princes known to me – who constituted the full interview panel. I was struck by this breach of professionalism, but I tried to respond with courtesy and a measure of grace. Several days of praise and persuasion, which continued even after it was acknowledged that I had not applied for the post concerned, followed. They tried every trick in the recruitment book to get me to agree to join them. This crossroads experience merely confirmed the Lord's purpose for me, and I resisted the pressure and declined the offer. Only three years earlier, I had faced perhaps the most trying crossroads experience of my career to date.

A prince with moral suasion: While I was dean of the business school in my university, I had been seconded to become the chief executive of Scotland's inward investment agency. This high-profile body was responsible for various international activities with which I was familiar, and I had been involved in its establishment several years earlier. As a Christian I was comfortable with this move because of my passionate belief that employment is such a vital part of realizing the potential of each individual. While I was in this post within the country's economic development agency, Margaret Thatcher, the then prime minister, announced a radical policy change. One of the results of this policy was the complex merger of this agency with a large, country-wide group of civil servants concerned with employment and training. In total some two thousand five hundred people were involved in the two organizations, and there was much uncertainty about the out-turn of this merger process. I agreed to extend my secondment for a set period of time to manage this transition. I was familiar with the issues and was viewed as someone who could be dispassionate about the change. As often happens in such situations, the organization began to depend on my leadership – simply because I was so involved in shaping the different dimensions of its future and because many other senior people would be leaving. A lengthy public consultation was involved, as well as a new act of parliament, restructuring of organizations, allocation of roles and functions, and so on. The crunch for me came when the senior posts in the new organization were being filled. After many months of prayer and no small amount of agonizing, I was convinced that God was guiding me away from holding a single executive post and towards a portfolio career. This form of "tent-making" would enable me to combine my professional life with greater freedom to contribute to a number of Christian ministries. I was at a crossroads, and although the way ahead looked more uncertain as far as earnings were concerned, I was quite certain about the Lord's purpose for my life. As often happens, however, the "prince" was of a different view. The chairman of the new organization, a powerful man that I respected, wanted me to lead it. It would be an understatement to say that he pressurized me to take this job. He used many tactics to try to persuade me, but ultimately he told me that it was my Christian duty not to leave this group of people who looked to me to take them into this uncertain future. This angle of attack both disturbed and hurt me – but it did not sway me. It helped me to see quite clearly that there are different types of "princes" – and I had already heard from the only one that mattered. I launched my portfolio life in the summer of 1990 and, although several princes have tried to divert me from this path, I have never regretted taking a new direction at that crossroads.

I have learned from these experiences and others that princes can be powerful, subtle and persuasive. As they single-mindedly pursue their own ends, they can be baffled by someone applying

Christian principles to career decisions – although they often end up respecting that person for so doing. They know exactly the "temptation buttons" to press. They detest not having their own way and can make others feel small when things do not go their way.

I have also learned that we do not always see the crossroads coming up ahead. We need to distinguish between those that are routine and those that really matter. Crossroads that are important require time and prayer. We cannot predetermine how much time or how much prayer, but princes will pressurize us to make decisions neglecting both of these important ingredients. I made the three decisions I presented above in ten minutes, one week and six months, respectively.

I have learned a lot about myself at every crossroads. Each decision required me to pause for two reasons. First, I reflected on the guidance that I had received to date about my life. Second, I considered if it had changed in any way. I learned, for example, that I would not make a career decision for money; if the Lord chose to bless financially (and he did), it would be a by-product of any success I might enjoy. I also came to see, as I faced different crossroads, that I needed to learn patience.

Crossroads experiences have also given me valuable insights into who God is. I have learned that although it was not his intention to keep me in the dark, it sometimes took time for me to see his light. I have seen time and again that he has a plan for all of us, but that we need to search for it and confirm it regularly. Ideally, we take time to do this before the next crossroads comes along – then we have something to work with.

REFLECTION:

Identify three "princes" who have, or have had (or have tried to have), a powerful influence on your life. You may have felt their influence in areas other than career choices, and their influence may not have been negative. How much influence have you allowed these "princes" to exercise at your crossroads experiences? How big or small a role in these decisions have you allowed God? Reflect and pray about your responses to these questions.

Back to basics

All Christians need to carefully consider how much trust we place in the men and women around us. It's not that we should never trust other people. As we have seen, our daily lives are built upon mutual trust. So the train driver, the suppliers of our food, the doctor that we consult and the teachers of our children are among the many people in whom we place trust. But trust in matters of faith, direction, stewardship and eternity is quite a different matter. When we face crossroads experiences we need to grasp the importance of the principle behind this verse: "Stop trusting in man, who has but a breath in his nostrils. Of what account is he?"[3] This truth calls us to reaffirm the basics of our relationship with the Lord. As you do so, consider the following elements of trust.

Stop trusting in man: The prophet Isaiah speaks in the context of a national setting which is not all that different from our own. The people in Judah were characterized by arrogance, materialism and secularism – and they placed a premium on their achievements. They had many appealing role models in terms of human success. But Isaiah gives good reason for his advice on where they should place their trust. "The arrogance of man will be brought low and the pride of men humbled; the LORD alone will be exalted in that day, and the idols will totally disappear."[4] All men and women are creatures, dependent upon air to breathe and subject to God's judgement. Ideas and innovation, wealth and possessions, power and influence they may have in abundance but, as in Isaiah's day, many have little room for God. Why would we trust such people?

Start trusting in that man: Here is the core of our theme text. "It is better to take refuge in the LORD than to trust in man."[5] God has designed us so that we function at our best when we are trusting in him, but we need to constantly refocus on God and turn away from the influences of the people around us. As

Augustine observed, "The most profound essence of my nature is that I am capable of receiving God." God has given us not only that capacity, but also a clear mandate about giving our full attention to him and his instructions. When God affirms Jesus at his baptism, for example, saying "This is my beloved son", he is telling us to listen carefully to him.[6]

Go, follow *that man:* But listening itself is not enough. We need to hear the power of the words and feel the love of the person. Besides, we only have the capacity to obey God by the indwelling of the Spirit. As John Blanchard says, "A Christian is not a person who has made a new start on life, but a person who has received a new life to start with." Hence the enthusiasm with which the New Testament church so often described their new faith relationship as "Christ living in them". The demands made of the follower are set out in this most radical of verses. "If anyone would come after me, he must deny himself and take up his cross and follow me."[7]

CASE STUDY: Nehemiah and the princes

We will look at different biblical crossroads experiences throughout the book, searching for practical lessons that we can apply to our own situations. The subject of our first case study is Nehemiah.

Read Nehemiah 1 – 2

The stimulus: Nehemiah held the favoured position of cupbearer in the household of Artaxerxes. In his role as confidante he had influence and some standing – even though he was an exile in Persia. His life was comfortable, and his career path appeared set for the foreseeable future. Then came the bad news from home. The returning survivors of the exile were reported to be in "great trouble and disgrace. The wall of Jerusalem is broken down, and its gates have been burned with fire."[8] The Lord often brings new facts to our attention, and sometimes part of his plan in doing so is to change our direction. Sometimes, however, we respond with resistance, deaf ears, hardened hearts and feet that are reluctant to walk another way. But Nehemiah was open to what God was saying and confronted an unexpected crossroads experience. Are you aware of a stimulus from the Lord that you are ignoring?

The struggle: Nehemiah received this news in December. For four months, until the following April, he struggled and prepared. "When I heard these things, I sat down and wept. For some days I mourned and fasted and prayed before the God of heaven."[9] Think about Nehemiah's situation for a moment. His mind was probably in turmoil with many different thoughts: "Whoever heard of an exiled servant asking for a sabbatical? What will the king say and do? It's not safe back in Jerusalem. The Lord can use me here just as well." His struggle ended with a fervent prayer, in which he acknowledged that God could use the king to enable him to follow God's call. "Give your servant success today by granting him favour in the presence of this man."[10] Nehemiah had a burden and he made a choice. He had to go back to Jerusalem.

The sequel: It was a capital offence to appear sad in the king's presence – yet that is exactly how Nehemiah appeared before him. The previous four months had prepared him for this potentially difficult conversation in which he would use his influential position for God. The king granted his request to return to Jerusalem. "It pleased the king to send me; so I set a time."[11] Not only did this particular "prince" permit Nehemiah to go, but he was also a great help along the way (it's amazing how God used, and continues to use, people in power for his own purposes). So Nehemiah set off for Jerusalem with an escort of soldiers, letters of safe passage and the promise of construction materials. In other situations where princes try to exert influence, they merely serve to help us to realize that the Lord has other purposes for us – as they have in my own case. In the months ahead, Nehemiah would have ample reason not to trust princes as he commenced his rebuilding work in Jerusalem. The neighbouring governors were hostile, and they used both mockery and force as weapons. He remained a man of honesty, focused on his duty, full of integrity in his motives and displaying practical godliness at all times. Nehemiah was empowered to serve God in mighty ways because he had made a difficult but godly choice at the crossroads.

REFLECTION:

Think of a time when you faced a difficult decision and identify these three phases of stimulus, struggle and sequel in your particular set of circumstances. How did God bring you to the crossroads? What did your struggle look like? Did you make the right decision? Why or why not? What can you learn from Nehemiah's experience that might help you at a future crossroads?

Since we will be looking at the Psalms throughout the book, each chapter will end with a section called "selah". The psalmist used this word to encourage his readers to "pause and consider" what they had been reading.

SELAH:

What have you learned about the power of princes at your crossroads experiences?

How can you apply these words from C.S. Lewis to the daily challenges that you face: "Relying on God has to begin all over again every day as if nothing had yet been done"?

Do you exert the power of a prince over someone else? How can you ensure that you use that authority wisely and well?

---

[1] Jn. 10:3.
[2] Jn. 6:68 (NLT).
[3] Is. 2:22.
[4] Is. 2:17,18.
[5] Ps. 118:8.
[6] Mt. 3:17.

[7] Mk. 8:34.
[8] Neh. 1:3.
[9] Neh. 1:4.
[10] Neh. 1:11.
[11] Neh. 2:6.

2

Check Your Compass Regularly

(The LORD says) "I have installed my King on Zion, my holy hill." (Ps. 2:6)

Outline

Just as a traveller might use a compass to find the way, we need to regularly check our spiritual compass throughout the journey of life.

Compass people: How should Christians set their course?

Case studies: Using and abusing a compass: Four types of compass readers.

Malfunctioning compasses: Biblical case studies: What can we learn from the mistakes of the Zebedee family, Peter, the guests at the feast and the disciples on the road to Emmaus?

Wisdom from Proverbs: How to set a compass: What does it mean to search, choose and focus your compass?

Compass people

We can choose to rely on any number of external factors to determine the direction of our lives – especially at a crossroads. Most of us wouldn't think of hill walking, orienteering or travelling to a remote location without a compass and a map. We would need to know where magnetic north is to be able to set our course correctly. Compass readings can be distorted by a range of environmental factors, however, and so deceive the user. And there is always scope for human error, too. Recently I heard about how the proud owner of a new Mercedes in Germany was so focused on the screen, with its global position satellite system and inbuilt compass, that he drove his vehicle off the road and into a canal. Christians, too, can easily miss the road through lack of attention – not least to the voice of the Lord.

I have always been fascinated by what people aim towards in their lives – their personal magnetic north. For some it is the realization of a burning ambition; for others it is wealth; for many it is a sense of fulfilment. A visit to any sports club or gym will remind us that health and fitness are also on this list of aims for some people. "Nothing wrong with any of that," you say. And I agree. But some people, including many Christians, are unidirectional – focused solely on their own personal compass points. We all need to check our spiritual compass at regular intervals. Part of acknowledging that Jesus is Lord means recalibrating our lives to the focal point of heaven's compass. The early disciples expressed this controversial truth well when they said, "there is another king, one called Jesus."[1] Are you allowing Jesus to move the needle of your compass and determine where it comes to rest? The nineteenth-century writer Horatius Bonar captured this thought

I dare not choose my lot
I would not if I might
Choose thou for me, my God
So I shall walk aright

The Bible addresses this issue with remarkable force and clarity. Psalm 2 describes the hostility of the nations against the Lord and his Anointed One – and God lays down the ultimate eternal benchmark. The nations may neither recognize nor acknowledge him at the present time, but he says: "I have installed my King on Zion, my holy hill . . . Ask of me, and I will make the nations your inheritance, the ends of the earth your possession."[2] Our world may have rejected Christ as Lord, but God has already placed him in ultimate authority. This principle lies at the very heart of the Christian faith. I once saw an advertisement in the *New York Times* with the following headline: "Sing along Handel – do it yourself Messiah". The ambiguity is striking in a world where many people will bow to any messiah but Christ.

With echoes of Psalm 2, Peter confronted the leaders of the Jewish nation: "Therefore let all Israel be assured of this: God has made this Jesus, whom you crucified, both Lord and Christ."[3] Paul, too, develops the same theme when he writes: "And he made known to us the mystery of his will according to his good pleasure, which he purposed in Christ, to be put into effect when the times will have reached their fulfilment – to bring all things in heaven and on earth together under one head, even Christ."[4] Paul uses a metaphor from Greek primary education here. Whereas we place the sum of a column of numbers at the bottom, they placed the sum at the head of the column. God has revealed to us that the Lord *is* the sum of all things, at the head of history. Why, then, do we not set our compass, the direction of our lives, according to him? As we will see, and as we know from our own hearts, there are many reasons we do not. None of our reasons are good ones – and none will stand up under God's scrutiny.

REFLECTION:

All heaven is waiting to help those who will discover the will of God and do it. (J. Robert Ashcroft)

Are there times when you should have checked your spiritual compass but decided that you would set your course towards another goal instead? How might things have been different if you had set Christ as your aim?

CASE STUDIES: Using and abusing a compass

As we flesh out this idea of how a Christian sets his or her spiritual compass, we consider the four basic types of compass reader in Table 2.1 and then in four different case studies. Look for characteristics of yourself here, rather than identifying others known to you.

Table 2.1 Four Types of Compass Reader

Optimizer:	Same direction, consulting several compasses
Dreamer:	Wild gyrations, no clear direction
Wanderer:	No evident direction of any kind, missing a compass
Follower:	Consistent direction, regular spiritual compass checker

Jordan – holding steady, consulting several compasses: Jordan grew up with strong Christian influence from his family and was a brilliant student. He chose to study medicine and excelled at it. He took all of the tough early qualification hurdles, demanding work and training schedules in his stride. Promotion followed promotion like clockwork as he became ever more absorbed in his career. He experienced various crossroads, including a health scare or two, but he single-mindedly pursued his path with little thought to other alternatives. His colleagues said that he was like a gyroscope – when set off balance he had an inbuilt tendency to bounce back to the vertical. He participated in a range of professional bodies connected with his chosen surgical specialization and travelled internationally. Because of his pioneering research he was in great demand as a recognized world authority on his subject. Although Jordan was a highly driven man, he was never quite sure about what drove him or where he was going. When pushed about his goals he would admit, "It's money to a large degree, but it's also recognition and striving for excellence in all that I do." If asked about the compass analogy, he would have said that he needed several. "I do acknowledge Jesus as Lord, but I'm not sure that really covers the other needs I have for goals to drive towards in the short- to medium-term. No, I don't have a problem with the fact that my spiritual and secular compasses might be incompatible – but I honestly don't think about it very much." He came across lots of Christians – both colleagues and patients – and many of them pressed him on matters of lifestyle. At times he was challenged and impressed by the fact that they had set the direction of their lives by different criteria. Jordan rationalized this by seeing his life in distinct phases – his twenties were for qualifying; his thirties for promotion; his forties for reputation; his fifties for status. His sixties were still an unknown, but he vaguely thought about community service – in which he included "church work". He admitted that this way of categorizing his life was his invention and that he had never consulted God about it. It was in fact his way of handling his restless conscience. He was now fifty-five, and he was beginning to wonder about the direction of his life, past and future. Was this a crossroads, he wondered?

Marina – wild gyrations, no clear direction: Marina was named "woman entrepreneur of the year" for her business prowess on several occasions. She was a serial entrepreneur and a self-styled, part-time Christian. She had made two fortunes by her early thirties, having established and sold first her chain of fashion shops, and then her logistics business which sourced garments from all over the world. At age thirty-four she launched her third business, marketing quality children's clothing over the internet. She was famous for having "the Midas touch" and investors clambered to support her. Like many entrepreneurs, Marina was a passionate, energetic, and charismatic lady who demanded much of herself and of all who worked with her. She was a "highs and lows" person, prone to mood swings and extreme reactions to situations. This is where the compass swings came in. She loved the passion of evangelical rallies and the fervour of some of the God channels on television. At times these would appear to draw her to the Lord and to bountiful acts of charity – but not with any consistency. Cynics among her peers would say, "Marina has made more public commitments to Christ than politicians have made promises – and they mean about as much!" She resented these comments but she had to admit that, for reasons she did not quite understand, success was actually her number-one driving force. If she had looked deep enough she would have seen that recognition was her adrenaline – she was driven by the power and standing that came with success. She made many public speeches on her business successes but never attributed anything to God. And then she came to a crossroads. Her new business venture was planned on a grand scale, with high-profile launches in London, Paris and New York. Convinced of her own infallibility, she had rejected investment offers from others and had grossly exposed her own capital to all the risks. She began to experience problems on all fronts – the technology was a failure, the product quality was variable, order fulfilment was poor and the customer base slow to develop. For the first time she was facing financial disaster and personal shame. After weeks of public speculation, the business failed. She felt totally directionless, yet she felt an inner longing to find her neglected spiritual north. But how? And would people say that she was just fleeing to a port in a storm?

George – no evident direction, missing a compass: The education system failed George. Although he attended good schools, he lacked motivation and none of his teachers managed to inspire him to take an interest in their subject. He liked music and sport, but little else. He was a Christian and not afraid to tell people about it. In fact, his faith was the only thing that he showed real enthusiasm about. This puzzled his teachers, who could see that he had ability but had no idea how to reach him. "These Christian youngsters are usually keen students – what makes him different?" they would wonder or, less charitably, "He takes the Christian thing too seriously – but obviously not the bit about using his talents wisely." He was pleasant, courteous and carefree. When he left school he drifted between jobs for several years. He stocked supermarket shelves, worked in a call centre, dug ditches and was a deck hand in a cruise liner. Most of his pay cheques financed his band, which played at Christian gigs across the country and had a small, select following. He thought that his music might open a way into a Christian ministry, but few others agreed with his own evaluation of his musical gifts. At twenty-four years of age George did wonder at times about his direction. But this was usually short-lived and he found new direction in a "new sound" for the band. His pastor and parents were increasingly concerned about where George was going. His father, a successful accountant, found relating to George increasingly difficult and the cause of growing stress in the home. His parents had taken the view that this was all a phase, however, and that something would come along to help him focus. It did, but unfortunately it was a drift towards the local drug culture. What began as a desire to help addicts became a rather too close involvement in some of their habits. George blamed it on the pressure that he felt to find himself and a direction for his life. This was his way to escape, but there was hope. Fortunately George understood the risks of his behaviour, and one day he found himself praying a simple prayer for the first time. "Lord, what do you want me to do?" George was approaching his first real crossroads experience.

Sarah – consistent direction, regular spiritual compass checker: It was not that Sarah was super holy, but she did seek the Lord's direction throughout the various phases of her life. It began with her conviction that she should be a teacher when all her close friends were going into other professions. She was tempted to stay with them through their post-school training, but she knew she wanted to follow a different path. She had benefited greatly from some godly school teachers and camp leaders, and she wanted to follow in their footsteps. She graduated with high honours in maths and physics, and major international companies recruiting at her university offered her attractive salaries if she would join their research teams. Her professors were equally keen to retain her in their labs – but to no avail. She was convinced that the Lord wanted her to teach. These lucrative alternatives did require her to check her compass again and again. There was glamour in being courted, and she was tempted by the idea of travel, foreign assignments and large salaries. She quickly established herself as both a good teacher and an enthusiastic leader. In every sense she was fulfilled in her role. In her early thirties she came to another crossroads. She was convinced that further career progression was not enough in itself. She had developed a keen interest in the HIV/AIDS crisis in southern Africa, and she had been corresponding with teams involved in work there. By this time she was teaching in an excellent school and set for early promotion to head of department – but Africa called. Another complication was that Douglas, her close companion and potential husband, did not share that call. For months they were both in an emotional maelstrom. And the compass needle did swing violently at times. Douglas was willing (but only just) to go, but Sarah wanted to work in the remote villages where he would be unlikely to find employment. Eventually it was all too difficult, and their relationship faltered and failed. Having completed preparatory nursing training, Sarah went to Africa. She felt the loss but was as convinced as ever that this was the Lord's plan. The work and the environment proved very challenging, but she was content. For the first year her health was poor, and there were many times when she needed to check her compass – especially when she felt the pull of friendships and the offers of posts back home "when she got Africa out of her system". That never happened. Over the following 20 years she experienced three civil wars, two major periods of famine and much personal deprivation – but she retained her initial conviction. And she kept checking her compass.

REFLECTION:

Is it too late for Jordan to take a new, God-informed direction? How would you counsel Marina? How would you advise George to proceed? What can you learn from Sarah and others like her?

A compass lesson: John Newton, of *Amazing Grace* fame, was an eighteenth-century slave trader, slave, villain and preacher. His epitaph records the dramatic effect of finding a new compass direction in Christ: "once an infidel and a libertine; preserved, restored, pardoned and appointed to preach the faith he had so long laboured to destroy". It's no wonder that he found grace amazing!

Malfunctioning compasses: Biblical case studies

The Bible offers us insight into the lives and circumstances of such a great variety of people that it is not surprising that these include many individuals with compasses that were clearly out of order. Inattention, ambition, misunderstanding, unsanctified priorities, pride and disorientation are among the many reasons for their malfunctioning personal compass needles. What can we learn from some of them?

The Zebedee family: It's not hard to see where James, John and their mother were coming from. They wanted a key family spot in the kingdom hierarchy. Their approach was not subtle: "Grant that one of these two sons of mine may sit at your right and the other at your left in your kingdom."[5] The two sons had attended many roadside seminars and workshops, seeing first-hand the spirit of service that was the hallmark of their master. Greatness lay not in the seat, but in the service. But what they saw and heard evidently had little impact on them that day. Nor did they seem to understand when Jesus reminded them that these positions were not his to fill – they belonged to the Father. "He was going to the Cross; they had their thoughts centred on self-advancement in the kingdom."[6] Jesus knew just how refocus them. "And whoever wants to be first must be your slave – just as the Son of Man did not come to be served but to serve, and to give his life as a ransom for many."[7] Try asking for a top kingdom spot after that comment . . . you can almost hear the sound of silence as the passage ends.

Peter in denial: Some people lose their direction under pressure as circumstances steer them off course and into territory where, very soon thereafter, they bitterly regret being. Peter had enthusiastically promised unwavering allegiance to Jesus. But fear caused his compass orientation to veer wildly such that he was able to say, "I don't know this man you're talking about."[8] The process of correction began immediately for Peter, instigated by both memory and remorse as the cock crowed and Jesus' prediction was fulfilled. "And he went outside and wept bitterly."[9] As Ivor Powell comments, "Somewhere in the city, he broke his heart and decided his world had ended. All thoughts of forgiveness were rejected; in any case, he could never face his Lord again."[10] Fortunately Peter's story does not end here. Memory and remorse prepared him for forgiveness and the call of love from the resurrected Lord. A bumper catch of fish and an early breakfast on the shore were the prelude to a life-changing conversation. Asked three times about his love for his master, he exclaimed, "Lord, you know all things; you know that I love you."[11] It is agape love that effects the change as Peter commits himself to a life reflecting his deep affection for Christ and his active exercise of that love on behalf of others. There is no more powerful force in the universe. If your compass needle is misdirected, the root of the problem may be a lack of love – but there is always a way back.

Discounted invitations: While we may be rather casual about our acceptance of, and attendance at, invited events, good practice in the cultural setting of the parable of the great feast was rather different. The tradition was that the day of a feast was formally set, and invitations were sent out and accepted – but the exact time on the appointed day was not announced. When that day came and everything was prepared, the servants were sent to summon the guests. To accept an invitation and then refuse to come on the day was a grave and serious insult. Jesus makes clear that this parable is about the feast in the kingdom of God. And three people, who had not recently consulted their compasses, refused to come to the feast.[12] The first offered a very twenty-first-century excuse. He had purchased a field that needed to be inspected, and so the claims of his business ranked above the claims of God. How much easier it is for men and women to be influenced by the power of assets than by the power of God's call. The excuse of the second was that something new had come along – in this case five yoke of oxen – and, of course, they had to be tried out. The power of novelty is great and capable of dramatically changing our focus – a new job, a new experience, a new friend, a new hobby, a new holiday home, or whatever. All of these things will take God's place and swing our compass needle if we let them. The third guest gave the excuse that he had just been married. He may have been sheltering behind an ancient Jewish privilege to stay at home with his wife for a year to avoid going to the feast.[13] There was nothing wrong with his wanting to be with his wife, but this desire appears to have crowded out his master. Sometimes the best of things can dull and distort the voice of the Lord. Isn't it amazing what we offer up to God as excuses for the quality of our discipleship?

Baffled disciples: In spite of the recent joy of the resurrection, the two disciples on the journey to Emmaus were baffled, wistful and reflective – God had evidently not done what they wanted. The Lord joins them and walks and talks with them – but they don't even recognize him. The compass needle is way off. Why? Were they simply walking west into the sun so they could not see him clearly? Was the Lord different in appearance? Were they not well informed about recent events? What we do know is that their eyes were opened as they ate together and, when they recognized him, Jesus disappeared. They were immediately refocused: "Were not our hearts burning within us while he talked with us on the road and opened the Scriptures to us?"[14] It's amazing what "burning hearts" can do. Jesus had made sense of the past, present and future. He had brought purpose back to their lives, and they wanted to respond in worship. As Robert Cabot said, "Worship renews the spirit as sleep renews the body." That was certainly their experience. Like the disciples, we need to understand the Scriptures. We will not recognize God unless we know how he has revealed himself to us in his word. Our spiritual compass will lack direction unless we set it by his word.

Wisdom from Proverbs: How to set a compass

The Old Testament is full of wisdom, and Proverbs in particular "summons us to think hard as well as humbly; to keep our eyes open, to use our conscience and our common sense, and not to shirk the most disturbing questions".[15] Proverbs 4 charts the journey of the person who wants to live a well-managed life for God. In three dimensions, it gives us great advice on how to both set and check our spiritual compass.

Search: Verses 1–9 reveal the secret of the life God blesses. "Lay hold of my words with all your heart; keep my commands and you will live."[16] The writer makes it abundantly clear that we have to really want this. And, if we decide to take it, it may cost us all that we have. Christ reiterates this call powerfully and clearly – but do we allow him that degree of influence in our lives?

Choose: Verses 10–19 identify two very different paths – the way of wisdom and the way of the wicked. We need to check our compass at this crossroads. Many of us know the joy of choosing the way of wisdom, but most of us have also strayed onto the alternative path – and have not always recognized what was happening. The descriptions of these two paths should make us think. "The path of the righteous is like the first gleam of dawn, shining ever brighter till the full light of day. But the way of the wicked is like deep darkness; they do not know what makes them stumble."[17]

Focus: Verses 20–27 call us to get the basics right. We too often forget the routine, "physical" aspects of Christian living – paying close attention to the activities of our hearts, mouths, eyes and feet. It all begins in the heart (or mind): "Above all else, guard your heart, for it is the wellspring of life."[18] The mind and the direction of the compass needle are inextricably linked. Jesus builds on this principle on many occasions. In the parable of the rich fool, for example, he says, ". . . a man's life does not consist in the abundance of his possessions."[19]

REFLECTION:

Proverbs 4 clearly tells us to search diligently, choose wisely and focus consistently. How might applying these principles have helped the Zebedee family, Peter, the guests at the feast and the disciples on the road to Emmaus? Now apply them to your own life. Do you search for Christ with all your heart, or is the cost too great? Are you choosing the path of wisdom or wickedness? Is your focus on God or on other things? What do your answers reveal, and what changes do you need to make?

SELAH:

What problems have you faced and what lessons have you learned at crossroads experiences? What do these reveal about your "spiritual compass"?

In the seventeenth century Angelus Selesius wrote: "The crossroads are down here: which way to pull the rein? The left brings you but loss, the right nothing but gain."

Is the magnetic pull of Jesus as strong as it was when you first became a Christian? If not, why not? How can you change your direction if you need to?

---

[1] Acts 17:7.
[2] Ps. 2:6,8.
[3] Acts 2:36.
[4] Eph. 1:9,10.
[5] Mt. 20:21.
[6] Kenneth S. Wuest, *Mark in the Greek New Testament* (Grand Rapids: Eerdmans, 1950), 210.
[7] Mt. 20:27,28.
[8] Mk. 14:71.
[9] Lk. 22:62.
[10] Ivor Powell, *Mark's Superb Gospel* (Grand Rapids: Kregel, 1985), 386,87.
[11] Jn. 21:17.
[12] Lk. 14:15–24; Mt. 22:2–14.

[13] Deut. 24:5.

[14] Lk. 24:32.

[15] Derek Kidner, *Wisdom to Live By* (Leicester: Inter-Varsity Press, 1985), 11.

[16] Prov. 4:4b.

[17] Prov. 4:18,19.

[18] Prov. 4:23.

[19] Lk. 12:15b.

3

Live by the Right Standards

*"...the LORD's delight is in those who honor him,
those who put their hope in his unfailing love."*
(Ps. 147:11, NLT)

Outline

As Christians we have to make numerous decisions, in every area of life, involving our standards and behaviour.

Standards and Christian consciousness: What are Christian standards? What are our attitudes to these standards?

Beware of relativism: Where does relativism come from? How can we prevent it from seeping into our behaviour?

Distinctives: Christ requires us to be distinctive in the following areas: family, work, national life, society and community, personal relations and in God's service.

The power to choose: A checklist: What are the five essential ingredients that enable us to choose to live by the right standards?

Standards and Christian consciousness

Christ calls us to live a distinctive lifestyle – in our attitudes, beliefs, habits and behaviour.[1] In a world in which Christian standards are all but alien, it can be very difficult to maintain these standards in our behaviour. "All of my friends live by their own standards – and most of them don't think Christian standards are either applicable or desirable." "Times have changed, and somehow we have to accommodate these changes – so I'm not sure what to believe any more about morality, sexuality and marriage." "I try to be salt and light in my community, but no one seems to be watching or listening." "I can take hostility directed towards my practice as a Christian, but I find indifference really difficult to cope with." Negative remarks such as these lack the confidence and authority of the Bible on this tough subject. We have no alternative but to model the Christian life, and so we need to continuously assess whether we are living each dimension of our lives by the "right" standards. When did you last think about this? Are there certain "no go" areas in your life, where Christian standards do not prevail? Are there areas where you do not want them to prevail?

Psalm 147:11, quoted above, reminds us of something remarkable. What delights you? A new convert? A glorious sunset? A beautiful garden? A victory by your favourite soccer team? A family member getting a good result in an examination? Good news about your health? An answered prayer? There are many possible answers here. But what about God? He delights in those who honour him. Sound improbable? Some of the struggles he witnesses as his followers try to meet his standards are feeble, some are ugly, some are beautiful, some are triumphant – but he delights in all of our faithful efforts. So be encouraged. Even when we ourselves don't find much personal delight in our past or current efforts, if our hearts are right God delights. And he always knows the heart. As we have seen, it is crucial that "Above all else, guard your heart, for it is the wellspring of life."[2] We will look in more depth at the vital subject of honouring God in Chapter 10.

Practising Christian standards presents "crossroads" challenges. God promises that, through all of them, "I will instruct you and teach you in the way you should go; I will counsel you and watch over you."[3] This close relationship with God entails our knowing what kind of behaviour he expects. Many of us ignore his instructions or choose which ones we will heed. With God's promises come responsibilities. So Paul writes, "For it was his will that we, who were the first to set our hope on Christ, should cause his glory to be praised".[4] We know that this will not happen apart from the power of God. But our responsibility is to know the Bible and use it as our frame of reference. What sort of impression are we making in our families or among our friends, peers and neighbours? To what extent are we really bringing him glory? Among other things, we need to be much more aware of the following:

- We display the standards by which we live every day, in a variety of routine behaviours. In the daily routine of life we may scarcely feel like we are making real choices about Christian standards. But we are.
- Others see patterns in our standards of behaviour before we do – and once they do, they have long memories.
- We rarely take the time to stop and evaluate the standards we have adopted in our lives to see if they match God's expectations.
- No one is perfect, but if we name Jesus as Lord we have no choice but to "speak Christian, and live Christian". You will search the Bible in vain for an "opt-out" clause so that you can practise your personalized version of Christianity. Jesus Christ is the sole designer.
- Many of our peers live moral lives and adopt high standards of behaviour without any basis of faith. Some of them put Christians to shame. It is imperative that we connect our high standards to their true source with the courage and confidence that can only come from the Spirit.

Table 3.1 summarizes the many different attitudes to Christian standards.

Table 3.1 Attitudes to Christian Standards

Adapters:	Recognize the teaching of the Bible but are inclined to modify it to suit their own ends – often because they see the biblical standards as being too demanding and unrealistic.
Compromisers:	Are always looking for a "middle way" that will prove more palatable – something that keeps the spirit but amends the letter. They are not concerned by double standards, which they usually explain away as being a result of changes in style and outlook.
Reformers:	Usually want to interpret the Bible in a new way to soften the blow of what God said because, after all, it was for a different era. They are inclined to say that the Bible is silent in areas where it speaks very clearly but does not say what they want.
Customizers:	Are rather keen on designing their own standards from scratch to suit specific situations. They are commonly found doing this in areas such as stewardship, morality and values – especially in a crisis at a crossroads. They are experts at rationalizing their own position and declaring that they have a clear conscience.
Adopters:	Understand the challenges of being Christian and the exacting nature of God's demands but know they can only meet them by the power of the Spirit. They regularly pray that they may be able to live by the right standards. God delights in them.

REFLECTION:

Dietrich Bonhoeffer said that

> Only he who believes is obedient; only he who is obedient believes.

Where do you see yourself in Table 3:1? Which of these attitudes would you regard as being consistent with true Christian faith? What sort of pressures would cause you to adopt an attitude that you know does not delight God?

Beware of relativism

While we can never use the environment in which we live for Christ as an excuse for our behaviour, we need to understand the forces working against us. I know I'm in trouble if I see a car driving towards me on my side of the carriageway. A pointed gun spells danger in anyone's language. While the forces of relativism, which has been called "the spirit of the age", are no less real, they are much more subtly deployed in the battle for our minds. Advocates of this way of thinking reject and mock the very idea of "right standards". But Christians know that there is absolute truth, and they should never be afraid to say so. C.S. Lewis wrote rather pointedly on the subject. "Some people prefer to talk of moral 'ideals' rather than moral rules and about moral 'idealism' rather than moral obedience."[5] The language of absolutes, of rules and obedience, brings many challenges.

Relativism is, quite simply, the belief that there are no absolutes in truth and morals. Standards are determined by a majority vote. Most Christians would say that relativism does not influence them in any way – but realism tells us otherwise. What, then, are the ingredients of this proposition called relativism, and how can we avoid being swayed by it? Every one of the five dimensions of this worldview in Table 3.2 threatens danger to the Christian.

Table 3.2 The basis of relativism

Focuses on the secular:	We see and take what we want, now. We do not worry about how, why, or the consequences. Spiritual considerations are irrelevant, or at best they are secondary. What we do (or who we are) is of no eternal value.
Discounts the past:	The truth of the past – in history, politics or religion – is suspect. The Bible could not be the inspired word of God.
Dismisses the supernatural:	Sees nothing beyond this world. Since all nature is equal, humankind could not be at the centre of God's plans. We are therefore entirely justified to live for the "here and now".
Assumes the best:	We were all born good and can solve the world's problems by our own efforts. Relativism sometimes claims that we are all our own gods, with supreme energy and innovative capacities to create our own new world. It rejects the idea than human beings are sinners and need a Saviour.
Relies on pragmatism:	Since there is no objective truth, each of us determines reality – if it works and feels good for you, it's fine. Neither God nor anyone else has any right to interfere with your decisions.

The Christian today walks through this landscape of relativism – these assumptions are part of the very air that we breathe. We all need to reflect on what inroads these influences have made, and are making, into our standards of behaviour. Although they rarely threaten to drive me into relativism, I confess to being vulnerable to several of these subtle and engaging influences. For example, I regularly patrol the frontier between pragmatism in business values and my Christian values in assessing people, making financial decisions and reacting to the behaviour of competitors. And, although as Christians we are to see the potential for good in those made in God's image, I have to be careful not to grace the best of men with divine qualities. Many of us also give far too little attention to the supernatural in terms of priorities for our use of time, resources and money.

I have come across many sad cases in which the influences of relativism have totally destroyed the witness of bright, strong and visible Christians. One, a brilliant lawyer, excellent communicator and former church leader, fell to sexual sin and was living a life of double standards. In so doing he destroyed his own testimony, his family and his children's faith. He also profoundly disturbed a group of young people that he led. I still grieve for him. We keep in touch, albeit with difficulty. I send him Christian literature and assure him of our prayers. As it happens, I met him in a garden centre as I was writing this chapter and told him about God's grace in my current illness – to his great discomfort, as he didn't want to hear about God's grace. I know, however, that the Father still loves the prodigal. Another victim of relativism I know is one of the brightest financial minds of his generation, a true workaholic whose god is money. His love of money led him to leave his wife and tiny baby for another partner. He had such potential for God, but he gave in to these forces of relativism at a time when we were working together. He kept his private life away from me and, when I tried to reach him, his rationalization for what had happened was quite extraordinary and totally self-justifying. We should never underestimate our capacity to rewrite God's rules. I have now lost touch with him, but he is still in my prayers. Sadly, I could fill a chapter with such examples. The devil is indeed like a "roaring lion". We all need to keep those we know who are similarly affected in prayer. Don't give up.

REFLECTION:

To which of the forces of relativism are you most susceptible in your present circumstances? As you pray for strength to maintain God's standards, think about what motivates your behaviour. Joni Eareckson Tada has wisely observed, "What if God arranged things so that we would experience a mild jolt of pain with every sin, or a tickle of pleasure with every act of virtue? Sort of a divine behaviour modification, if you will. Would you obey because you loved God? I don't think so. I think that you'd obey simply because you desired pleasure and not pain."

Distinctives

The Bible gives clear pictures of what a faith-based life looks like in the real world. We need to make choices regarding our standards in many different areas of life, and in all of them we are to be distinctive in a Christlike way. Before we look at some of these, we need to establish some of the foundational principles that govern all Christian behaviour. Paul writes about some of these principles in Galatians. "The entire law is summed up in a single command: 'Love your neighbour as yourself.'"[6] "So I say, live by the Spirit, and you will not gratify the desires of the sinful nature. For the sinful nature desires what is contrary to the Spirit, and the Spirit what is contrary to the sinful nature."[7] "But the fruit of the Spirit is love, joy, peace, patience, kindness, goodness, faithfulness, gentleness, and self-control. Against such things there is no law."[8] If we truly lived by these principles, I would not need to write more on this topic. God's intention for us is that, through the powerful and active coaching of the Spirit, we would choose the right standards.

God expects us to be distinctive in the following six areas. In each area we will consider the standards of two biblical characters. Many of them reached crossroads experiences at which they had to make crucial decisions regarding standards that had far-reaching effects.

In the family environment: The Bible sets high standards for both husbands and wives in terms of love, submission, respect and faithfulness, and for children in areas such as obedience, honour and respect.[9] The Christian family is to provide a unique showcase for the practice of Christian faith throughout the ups and downs of life. At its best, it is a glorious model; at its worst, breakdown takes on tragic proportions. David, for example, variously commended as a man after God's heart, warrior, musician, saint and prophet, also displayed vulnerability in family matters. He stained his character by the deceitful way he seduced Uriah's wife, Bathsheba, and took action that led to her husband's death.[10] His subsequent grief was profound, as was his humbling of himself before God. We can glimpse his sorrow and hear his cry for pardon in his psalms.[11]

David also faced other serious family problems with his son Absalom. His third son, his favourite and likely heir, had physical beauty, elegance and persuasiveness on his side. Yet he turned out to be a traitor, murderer and egotist with little thought or feeling for anyone else. While some of those around Absalom had faith and brought some restraint to his conduct, he did not share their theology and behaved in a godless manner. Absalom's standards were his own, in spite of his upbringing and privileges.[12]

Christians today face many other types of "family" issues – including the redefinition of the nuclear family itself, which is in decline in many countries in the west. Extending Christian care both to, and within, single parent families is vital but sometimes difficult. Another challenge is the absence of family links – not just for the aged, but for a new generation of lonely, professional singles who have deferred marriage and children and who end up with neither.

In the workplace: The Bible presumes that Christians will recognize God as a co-worker in the workplace. Work for the

Christian is a calling, a form of stewardship, a dimension of service, and above all brings glory to God.[13] When we apply God's standards, we bring glory to him. The parable of the rich fool is a classic illustration of applying the wrong standards in the workplace.[14] Jesus cautions against greed here, which he recognizes as one of the key perils in the market-place. Christians need to remember how dangerous it is. This skilled and highly successful farmer, doubtless an agrarian trendsetter in his community, displays great business acumen in his foresight, planning and energy. He needed adequate and secure storage for all of his grain and many goods. Was he not being wise? Indeed he was – but then we read on to discover that he was planning his future on purely secular terms. His provision and horizons are purely physical. The spiritual content is zero. Towards God, he had no riches. This is a salutary lesson, and a sharp reminder of the endgame towards which so many affluent and greedy Christians can drift.

Philemon and Onesimus provide a more positive biblical example.[15] Philemon, probably a convert of Paul's, was a freeman, slave owner and leader who lived in Colosse. Onesimus, his slave, had escaped from Asia to Rome and probably stole money to make this possible. He met Paul, was converted, changed and proved to be very useful in his work. But Onesimus belonged to his master, Philemon, and Paul had to encourage him to put his past wrongs right. In an act requiring considerable grace on Philemon's part, Paul sent Onesimus back to Colosse with Tychicus. Paul knew and respected Philemon and had confidence that he could ask him to regard the former slave as a partner in Christ. Paul also prayed that his own heart might be refreshed in Christ as a result of the way Philemon receives Onesimus. There are great lessons in grace here. The offence and the disruption are to be forgotten, the slave is now a brother.

As John Stott puts it, "Grace is love that cares and stoops and rescues".

There are lessons in forgiveness here, too. The slave had no right of asylum, but the owner had the right to kill or disfigure him on his return. C.S. Lewis reminds us that "If God forgives us, we must forgive others. Otherwise it is almost like setting up ourselves as a higher tribunal than him." Finally, this story models restoration – finding a way back is never easy, and the godly response required love, not regulation or convention. What a difference love made at this crossroads in the lives of both Onesimus and Philemon.

In national life: Leaders who pay homage to God are expected to rule with justice, even-handedness and integrity. Yet we find many examples of the opposite, both in biblical characters and in contemporary society. Jeroboam, Solomon's son and successor, comes to mind.[16] After his father's death, he split the kingdom and became the first king of the ten tribes of Israel. In order to please his people he abandoned the commandments and promises of God and set up golden bulls for worship. Indeed, he required this form of worship from his people. The consequences of his actions continued long after his death as many subsequent kings perpetuated this national idolatry. History remembers him as the man who made Israel sin. He gave the people a false religion and led them to live by standards that were wholly hostile to their heritage as God's chosen people.

Gideon, the judge and mighty warrior, set an example of godly leadership.[17] One of the brightest lights in Old Testament history, Gideon judged Israel for some forty years. He emerged from poverty to noble service, rid his father's house of idols, laid a fleece before God to confirm his mission, chose a handful of men to fight a horde of Midianites and was tough with those who resisted him. We can learn much from his devotion and obedience to God.

Those who are in leadership set the tone for the nations or organizations they lead. Yet many Christian leaders I know want to be secret disciples and are not prepared to acknowledge their faith in public. Some of them live by the highest Christian standards but don't attribute them to Christ. This has long puzzled me. Such behaviour has major consequences for Christian witness: it reduces the number of role models for successive generations; it results in apparent under-representation of the cause of Christ in influential circles; it reduces the volume of the "Christian voice" in our society and so on.

In society and community: None of us live in a vacuum. God asks us to take our places in a diverse range of roles in society – whether these roles are formal or informal, paid or unpaid, low-profile or high-profile, home-based or in the market-place, and so on. Every one of us has a place, and God expects us to live as Christians wherever we are. Although biblical characters may appear larger than life, they still have much to teach us in our humble slots. Elisha, for example, Elijah's companion and successor, became a great moral leader.[18] He emerges as a man of God with indomitable faith, great courage, deep sympathy, clear understanding and remarkable foresight. He asked for, and received, a double portion of Elijah's spirit. What do we seek by way of empowerment from God for our daily practice of his standards?

Hezekiah's story, on the other hand, is a mixed one – a bit like many of ours.[19] He was one of the best kings Judah ever had and he showed great faith. He was sincere and devout, but not perfect. God enabled him to overcome his upbringing under his wicked and apostate father Ahaz. Supported by Isaiah, the community experienced religious revival in his early reign. During a period of illness Hezekiah asked God for a longer life and, through Isaiah, God granted him 15 years. He did not make good use of these years, however. Manasseh, his son and heir, was born during these years and was a total disaster as a king. Divine blessing, vanity and self-sufficiency led Hezekiah astray into pride, and he subsequently lost favour with God as he became obsessed with his household treasures. Having passed with flying colours at the crossroads, where he rejected the idolatry of his father, he failed in his crisis with prosperity. Sound familiar?

In personal relations: There is no better benchmark of our behaviour than the fruit of the Spirit, as we saw above. We can only aspire to this quality of personal relationships in all of the contexts in which we interact with people. All of us have gaps to fill and situations to remedy. If you want to study an enigma in personal relations, look at Jacob.[20] Rather like Dr Jeykll and Mr Hyde in Robert Louis Stevenson's story, Jacob is both good and bad – a man of both guile and prayer. He deceived his father, Isaac, to gain his blessing and Esau's birthright. But he also had remarkable spiritual experiences at Bethel and Peniel. On his second visit to Bethel he led his family to purge themselves of their foreign gods and built an altar to God. Renamed Israel, he received a history-transforming promise. "And God said to him, 'I am God Almighty; be fruitful and increase in number. A nation and a community of nations will come from you, and kings will come from your body. The land I gave to Abraham and Isaac I also give to you, and I will give this land to your descendants after you.'"[21] We can take encouragement from this man – he had feet of clay, but in God's grace he sired the sons who became the foundation of a nation.

The story of Lot gives us another example of complex broken relationships. Lot had a truly worldly mind that influenced both his choices and his personal relationships.[22] Lot and his uncle, Abraham, travelled together and came out of Egypt to the Bethel area with considerable wealth. Quarrels among their herdsman meant that they had to separate. Lot's choice of land for himself was a bad and selfish one, ignoring his elder uncle's right to first choice. He chose the fruitful, fertile land with disastrous consequences. He chose the direction of Sodom, a city that was soon in his soul. He lost his wife and his wealth and sacrificed his influence in that city. His is another sad story of ambition and avarice taking over in a life that began faithfully enough. There are many Lots out there today – how can you avoid becoming one of them?

In God's service: The New Testament is full of guidance on discipleship, church life and Christian service. Christian service and obedience are to flow out of gratitude and love for our Master. As Oswald Chambers says, "It seems amazingly difficult to put on the yoke of Christ, but immediately we do put it on, everything becomes easy." The story of Demas teaches us about the consequences of an abandoned yoke and lowered standards. Demas was one of Paul's companions during his first Roman imprisonment. We have little knowledge of his life or the reasons he fell. Perhaps he was seduced by the wealth and glitter of the capital city. Perhaps he decided that the sacrificial life of the prisoners would be too much for him to bear. Was this painful and risky path really for him? Surely Paul and the others didn't deserve this reward for their loyal behaviour? Is it all worth the effort? He probably struggled with questions like these before he made the choice that Paul records in heartbreaking language. "For Demas, because he loved this world, has deserted me and has gone to Thessalonica."[23] The line between occupation and preoccupation with our world is always a fine one, and this man slipped over the edge.

Luke's story is very different. We know little of his Gentile background, but his very name (meaning "light giving") reflects the quality and consistency of his service for the Lord. A man of learning and knowledge, he was a precise observer and accurate recorder. His two books reflect these skills and his fine touch with language. The beloved physician, Luke gave his best to service – and we benefit from that service to this day. Does the standard of our service mirror the resources and talents we possess – or is it poor reflection of a heart not entirely devoted to God?[24]

REFLECTION:

In the seventeenth century William Temple wrote, "If Christianity has never disturbed us, we have not yet learned what it is."

Do some prayerful self-evaluation in each of these six areas, as they are relevant to your circumstances. For example, what element of Christian practice distinguishes you in your community? In the church, what do you do to encourage (or discourage) others? What do you do to add to, or subtract from, the Christian focus of your family unit?

The power to choose: A checklist

We don't have the power in ourselves to live by God's standards, but God does give us the power to choose. In *The Message*, Eugene Peterson's paraphrase of the Bible, we read

> . . . thank God! In the Messiah, in Christ, God leads us from place to place in one perpetual victory parade. Through us, he brings knowledge of Christ. Everywhere we go, people breathe in the exquisite fragrance. Because of Christ, we give off a sweet scent rising to God, which is recognized by those on the way of salvation – an aroma redolent with life. But those on the way to destruction treat us more like the stench from a rotting corpse.
>
> This is a terrific responsibility. Is anyone competent to take it on? No – but at least we don't take God's Word, water it down, and then take it to the streets to sell it cheap. We stand in Christ's presence when we speak; God looks us in the face. We get what we say straight from God and say it as honestly as we can.[25]

2 Corinthians 2:14–17 is the Christian's job description. In order to do our job effectively, we have to work through this checklist of choices. The choices are ours alone.

Be thankful: Thankfulness is a basic building block for applying Christian standards. We have to be thankful regardless of our circumstances – if we aren't thankful, then our behaviour will never glorify God because it will be based on looking to someone or something other than God. If we are bitter about our situation, God is unlikely to use that spirit to his glory.

Be victorious: Paul refers here in 2 Corinthians to the awe-inspiring triumphal processions that honoured victorious army generals. These generals received one or two in a lifetime, but we are part of one every day because God is at the head of the column as the ultimate victor empowering his followers.

Be fragrant: Christians are compared here to incense pots that were part of the procession. We need to leave a fragrance that is sweet, for it lingers long after we have gone.

Be strong: Our relationship with God determines every aspect of our behaviour. We cannot simulate or manufacture this strength. No one is competent without the power of the Spirit.

Be true: We need to live with integrity – we are not to be like the false prophets here who watered down the Bible to make it more palatable.

Living according to this checklist may mean sacrificing worldly success. Oswald Chambers said that

> We are not called to be successful in accordance with ordinary standards, but in accordance with a corn of wheat falling into the ground and dying, becoming in that way what it never could be if it were to abide alone.

We will return to this issue of success in the next chapter.

SELAH:

> Holy is the way God is. To be holy he does not conform to a standard. He is that standard. (A.W. Tozer)

How would you rate yourself in terms of adherence to Christian standards? How have your attitudes and behaviours changed over the years – for better or worse?

Can you identify crossroads at which you made life-shaping choices about the standards you planned to adopt? How have these decisions enhanced or detracted from your Christian witness?

---

[1] Neil Hood, *Whose Life Is it Anyway?* (Carlisle: Authentic Lifestyle, 2002), 6–13.

[2] Prov. 4:23.

[3] Ps. 32:8.

[4] Eph. 1:11–12 (NEB).

[5] C.S. Lewis, *Mere Christianity* (Glasgow: Collins, 1952), 65.

[6] Gal. 5:14.

[7] Gal. 5:16,17.

[8] Gal. 5:22,23.

9   See Eph. 5:22–33; 6:1–4; Col. 3:18–21.

10   2 Sam. 11.

11   As evidenced in Pss. 32 and 51.

12   2 Sam. 13 – 18. For a recent thought-provoking study of David, see Rebecca Manley Pippert, *A Heart for God* (Downers Grove, IL: IVP, 1996).

13   The subject of Christians and work is extensively covered in Neil Hood, *God's Payroll: Whose Work Is it Anyway?* (Carlisle: Authentic Lifestyle, 2003).

14   Lk. 12:13–21.

15   Philemon.

16   1 Kgs. 12 – 14.

17   Judg. 6 – 8.

18   2 Kgs. 2 – 13.

19   Hezekiah appears in many places in the Old Testament – see, e.g. 2 Kings, 1 and 2 Chronicles, Jeremiah, Hosea and Micah.

20   Gen. 25 – 33; 46 – 49.

21   Gen. 35:11,12.

22   Gen. 13 – 19.

23   2 Tim. 4:10.

24   I found Herbert Lockyer, *All the Men of the Bible* (Grand Rapids: Zondervan, 1958), helpful when studying these biblical characters.

25   2 Cor. 2:14 – 17 (*The Message*).

4

Use God's Benchmarks for Ambition and Success

"Teach us to number our days aright, that we may gain a heart of wisdom." (Ps. 90:12)

Outline

Measuring our success can be both controversial and personal — especially when we look at our lives according to the biblical standards for our effectiveness as disciples.

Ambition and success: *Keeping the score*: What is the difference between secular and real success?

The search for principles: What are the five biblical principles that will help us to recalibrate in order to measure success and ambition by Christian standards?

God-approved ambition: Godly ambition, the Christian's motivation and the ambitions that lead to "greatness" in the Bible and church history.

Unapproved: Selfish ambition: Why is ungodly ambition dangerous, and how do know if our ambitions are selfish?

True success: Its reality and visibility: How does Jesus model the roots of true success?

Ambition and success: Keeping the score

Ambition is a strong desire or drive for success, power, money, position, recognition or some other goal. Derived from a Latin word meaning "to go around" canvassing for votes, the word has its roots in the search for recognition and adulation. Measuring success, the product of their ambition, is for many people *the* consuming interest. Since to pursue success too overtly is regarded as crass, vulgar or unacceptable in respectable company, many people (and especially Christians) deny their drive to succeed. Meanwhile, each of us keeps score. While we like to think that we set our own performance criteria, most of us are in fact greatly influenced by our peers. So we measure our success by promotions attained, money invested, homes owned, cars driven, jewellery worn, social status enjoyed, public recognition commanded, positions held and so on. Few, if any, of us can claim that we are unaware of our relative position in these areas. Some people care much more about these things than others – some burn with jealousy, some are bitter, others are cynical, but only a few are indifferent. As we saw in Chapter 3, this is one of the areas in which relativism takes its toll on Christian minds. We all use the world's benchmarks to some degree, but some of us completely ignore God's benchmarks. It is possible for a Christian to be an expert at charting ambition and measuring secular success, but a novice in recognizing or measuring real, biblical success. How can this be?

Secular success: The world sets, and almost universally adopts, the criteria for success. These criteria are more quantitative than qualitative; the media widely and consistently promotes them; consumers pursue and reinforce them. Others measure us by these criteria –whether or not we choose to adopt them for ourselves – and their perspective on our lives sometimes influences us, albeit subtly or subliminally.

Real success: In contrast, spiritual criteria are counter cultural, long-term and appear intangible, even to many Christians. These criteria are entirely qualitative; they are inconsistent with secular measures; and it is easy for us to defer, postpone or reject them for a time. Some Christians do not want to face up to how poorly they perform by these standards, while others do not appear to understand real success since they apply the world's criteria in Christian contexts.

Daily I see and hear the evidence that Christians are ignoring God's benchmarks of ambition and success. "I can only quantify my success the way everybody else does – to do otherwise would divert my focus. I can't handle two sets of measures." "I'm terrified to apply biblical principles. I'm not a strong enough Christian to survive a probe of my ambitions and motives." "I'm not convinced of the validity of these two different ways of measuring success. Anyway, that's a matter for the theologians to sort out – I'm getting on with my life and, by any standards, it's a great success." "I couldn't handle the people and problems I'd have to face if I was more involved in Christian service. I know I handle tough problems and awkward people all the time in my senior position – but that's different. I'm in control." Have any of these unhealthy attitudes seeped into your thought processes?

We will explore different principles and characters in this chapter to discover all that we can about the spiritual benchmarks of success. But we need first of all to recognize that such benchmarks exist and to be willing to commit to apply them. In the secular context, few of us would question the examinations and training required to attain professional status or the fact that we need to accumulate experience before we look for career advancement. In other words, we readily accept that we need to achieve certain standards to realize our secular ambitions. What's different in the spiritual setting? Is it that we have lost our spiritual ambition? Do we think that we can meet God's standards without effort or willpower? Have we ever even had a passion to achieve things for God in the first place?

The search for principles

The following five verses will help us begin to recalibrate our ambitions and definition of success according to God's standards.

The list of principles they contain is not exhaustive, but these verses give us a thought-provoking start.

Count the days: There is a paradox at the centre of most of our lives. We live as slaves to both the calendar and the diary but fail to "count the days" in the terms of Psalm 90:12. Counting the days in this way means standing back from the routine of each day or week and asking questions. "What have I achieved for God in my life?" "What am I planning to achieve with the time I have left?" "What has God taught me so far?" The promise is that, if we do this, "we may gain a heart of wisdom". Few of us consistently fulfil this condition, and we are the poorer for it. As I will explain in Chapter 11, I have had occasion to think very hard about this issue.

Check your motives: What can we learn from Jeremiah's advice to his loyal secretary and scribe Baruch? "Should you then seek great things for yourself? Seek them not."[1] The Christian's standard defence is that all we are doing at all times is for the Lord and his glory. I have claimed this myself at times when it was not *wholly* true – I was doing what I planned, climbing certain ladders, realizing personal ambitions – and not always checking that this was what God wanted. The "great things" can easily be for ourselves, so it is essential to check our motives. This is tough because we are not always honest, and we can go to considerable lengths to deceive ourselves. While the process of purifying our motives is emotionally painful, it is essential. We will return to this question in more detail in Chapter 7.

Guard your mind: Paul warns us to "See to it that no-one takes you captive through hollow and deceptive philosophy, which depends on human tradition and the basic principles of this world rather than on Christ."[2] He was not talking about ambition as such, but about different theories that diverted Christ's followers in his day – things that hijack our minds, and ambition is one of those things. There are few stronger drives founded on the "basic principles of this world" than all-consuming, unsanctified ambition in the heart of a Christian. Today many of these ideas reach us through the secular media and, in subtle disguise, through some training and development materials that are riddled with New Age philosophies emphasizing the primacy of the individual in all things.

Follow the Name: John testified to the work of a group of itinerant evangelists and teachers with these words: "It was for the sake of the Name that they went out, receiving no help from the pagans."[3] Life today is complex. And if it isn't, we usually try to make it so. You might want to argue that although that was a fine principle for such a unidirectional and focused group, it's too simplistic for the twenty-first century. "How could I adjust my ambitions to go through that filter or meet that standard?" Have you ever tried? And if you have, did you do it in your own strength or commit your efforts to God, seeking his empowerment? Most people I meet who make such remarks have done neither. After all, we have committed our future to the Lord – and our ambitions are a big part of that future. Do your ambitions for life pass the "Name test"? Are they aspirations that are consistent with bearing Jesus' name? Do they reflect qualities of God's character? Will they bring him honour?

Engage in the Father's business: This principle derives from the young Jesus' words in response to his anxious parents who were searching for him, "'Why did you seek me? Did you not know that I must be about my Father's business?' But they did not understand the statement which he spoke to them."[4] Jesus was wholly committed to the work of redemption – a unique part of his Father's business that only he could do. But he also gave each of his followers a commission to continue this business of kingdom building, having assured them that "All authority in heaven and on earth has been given to me."[5] With this guarantee of power and the gift of the Holy Spirit we are enabled to "go into all the world". What part does the "Father's business" play in your busy work schedule? We are called to be ambitious for God in this area, using as much of our energy and skill as possible.

REFLECTION:

> There are two great days in a person's life – the day we are born
> and the day we discover why. (William Barclay)

Think about the ambition and success criteria that you have
been using on both your secular and spiritual scorecards. Are
you satisfied with these criteria? How can you reshape your
ambitions by applying these five principles?

God-approved ambition

We have seen that ambition comes in several forms, not all of
which are acceptable to God. All of us have made choices about
our ambitions – perhaps at a crossroads where the decision
point was not obvious. The alternatives are set out overleaf,
beginning with the good news.

1. Godly ambition

We should start by setting the record straight – Jesus never
undermined ambition. Nor did he try to discourage it in his
disciples, but he did appeal to them to display a very different
kind of ambition from that prevailing in the world around them.
In God's kingdom, greatness was to be found in humble service –
although he has always set stretching targets for that service. As
Jesus reminded the disciples, so he reminds us: "You know that
the rulers of the Gentiles lord it over them, and their high officials
exercise authority over them. Not so with you. Instead, whoever
wants to become great among you must be your servant, and
whoever wants to be first must be your slave – just as the Son of
Man did not come to be served, but to serve, and to give his life
as a ransom for many."[6] Jesus acknowledged that some would
want to be first (or great), and he did not criticize their aspirations.
But he set a high hurdle before them. The love of power had to
be set against the power of love. Many of his disciples achieved
greatness by his standards and, as the portraits in Table 4.1
remind us, this did not end in the first century. Helen Keller
reflected on the cost of greatness with these words: "Character

cannot be developed in ease and quiet. Only through experience of trial and suffering can the soul be strengthened, ambition inspired, and success achieved." No one has ever achieved spiritual ambitions without problems, criticism and opposition.

Table 4.1 The ambitions of some Christian "Greats"[7]

AUGUSTINE, BISHOP OF HIPPO (354–431): One of the most influential figures in early Christianity, Augustine was converted at age thirty-two from a life of debauchery and licentiousness. From 396, as Bishop in Hippo in North Africa, he used his position to preach, write extensively and combat widespread heresy. He faced many barriers and much hostility in the pursuit of these goals. His contributions were especially important for future generations of Christians, both in his stout defence of the gospel of grace and in his work that distinguished between the impermanence of the city of Rome and the eternal standing of the City of God.

MARTIN LUTHER, FATHER OF THE REFORMATION (1483–1546): A great man of God, Luther spent his life bringing the church back to its gospel beginnings. Following the shock of a friend's fatal accident, he abandoned the idea of a career in law and joined an Augustinian monastery. He quickly came to the conclusion that the church had lost the key to the kingdom. Luther came to faith through rediscovering these memorable words, which in turn shed a new light for him on the whole of Scripture: "For in the gospel a righteousness from God is revealed, a righteousness that is by faith from first to last, just as it is written: 'The righteous will live by faith.'"[8] His battles against papal authority were fierce and his persistent bravery in the face of all kinds of threats and pressures was remarkable.

HUDSON TAYLOR, FOUNDER, CHINA INLAND MISSION (1832–1905): From early childhood, Taylor declared that he wanted to be a missionary in China. However, his subsequent poor health made the realization of this ambition seem improbable. But his conversion at age seventeen confirmed his decision for China, and he studied medicine in preparation. He moved to China, aged twenty-one, in 1853. He fully adopted the Chinese style of living and was financially independent, depending on God for the provision of money and resources. By 1865, some eighteen missionaries had joined him and the China Inland Mission was established. By 1884 there were over eighty missionaries and an equivalent number of Chinese helpers, and by 1890 there were over one thousand. Taylor confronted numerous difficulties in this pioneering work, including those from enemies and civil unrest. The Boxer Rebellion in 1900 resulted in many missionary deaths. Taylor was once quoted as saying that he had met people who said, "Trusting God is a beautiful theory, but it won't work." He responded, "Well, thank God, it has worked and it does work."

BILLY GRAHAM, EVANGELIST AND CHRISTIAN STATESMAN (b. 1918): Billy Graham has made a massive contribution to re-establishing evangelism at the core of Christian thought and teaching. From humble beginnings in a Christian family in North Carolina, he was converted at age sixteen. He was convinced of his call to ministry and, after a period of training, pastoral work and crusades, he formed the Billy Graham Evangelistic Association in 1950. One of the amazing aspects of this organization has been that several of its core leaders have worked together ever since in the implementation of a global programme of evangelism. Often criticized for the "crusade" methodology, for his fundamentalist ministry, the lack of social gospel content and his statesman role with politicians, Graham has survived it all and experienced much evidence of God's blessing on his work. Not only have great numbers been added to the kingdom through his work, but he has also had a major impact on church and para-church Christian leadership across the globe. Although he would probably reject the concept, his global profile has meant that he has become the "representative" Christian of our day.

Many of these people received a unique call from God that totally changed their ambitions, although they could not have seen at the time how God would use them. Would you recognize and acknowledge such a call in your own life? Remember that the days of Christian "greats" are not over – whether on a local, national or international scale.

REFLECTION:

Think about those who have mentored and encouraged you on your Christian journey. What aspects of "greatness" have you observed in their ambitions and the way they have measured their success? What kind of advice have they given you when you faced crossroads decisions? What kind of impressions in this area of success are you leaving with people who regard you as a role model?

2. Motivation is everything

Ambition is not the problem, but what fuels it and directs it can be. Sorting out the complexity of our motives is not easy because of the presence of sin. At best we are broken and flawed people under reconstruction. Even a short time spent in self-examination reveals that our intentions are seldom totally pure. It's then that our expertise in disguising our real ambition kicks in, often clothed in high-sounding and creative spiritual language. But neither should we be paranoid about our motives and so sensitive that we end up doing nothing for God. The Lord knows our hearts – and that's always a great consolation. It is encouraging to find that even Paul felt uncertainty about his motives. "I care very little if I am judged by you or by any human court; indeed, I do not even judge myself. My conscience is clear, but that does not make me innocent. It is the Lord who judges me."[9] We can all identify with that tension between conscience and innocence. But, like Paul, we also need to recognize that there is a final arbiter of motives – and he's not one of our peers. Paul sets out three ingredients of godly ambition that need to be woven into the fabric of our lives and should govern all dimensions of a Christian's ambition. Without the three ingredients in Table 4.2 our ambitions can only be ungodly.

Table 4.2 Paul on godly ambition

Please God: "So we make it our goal to please him, whether we are at home in the body or away from it."[10] The moral here is simply this – if you have little desire to please God, you have to ask just how much you love him. As we shall see later, selfish ambition is based on love of self, not of Christ or of another. "For even Christ did not please himself but, as it is written: 'The insults of those who insult you have fallen on me.'"[11]

Preach Christ: "It has always been my ambition to preach the gospel where Christ was not known, so that I would not be building on someone else's foundation."[12]
All of us are with people and in situations every day where "Christ is not known". Our constant challenge is to make it our ambition to advance their knowledge of him through word and deed.

Portray Christ: "Make it your ambition to lead a quiet life, to mind your own business and to work with your hands, just as we told you, so that your daily life may win the respect of outsiders and so that you will not be dependent on anybody."[13] I personally struggle with this verse since I have not lived a quiet life by any standards. Nor have I made a particularly good job of minding my own business – as my many public commentaries on economic matters in the press, on radio and TV would evidence. Nor have these been my ambition, in all honesty – I am too interested in what goes on in the real world. Yet I am totally committed to portraying Christ by whatever means – and I have a lot

to learn about a quiet life! The point is well
made here that we need a measure of
quietness to focus on our godly ambitions,
and Satan is an expert at enticing us to
become busy fools.

Before we leave the issue of motivation, we should be clear on another important matter. The Lord needs ambitious disciples. He needs people of all kinds who make the best use of all the resources with which he has equipped them. And he needs them to succeed in their chosen professions, to take his name into places of influence throughout our societies, to fulfil the "salt and light" mandate. So, in principle, there are no "glass ceilings" through which we cannot rise – and ambition is essential to do this. But, as we have observed, the Christian's ambition is to be a governed and tempered one. At all times we are serving another Master. The one thing we should never do is to partition our "secular" and "spiritual" ambitions into separate compartments. Daniel, Joseph and Moses are all good biblical examples of this – they all reached the top in adverse environments but never denied their calling. That is our challenge, and it's a very difficult one. Tony Campolo says that "two dangers threaten the survival of Christendom – the one is mediocrity, the other success".[14] With God it is possible to rise above mediocre Christian commitment and achieve excellence in his cause. It simply can't be done without him. But we should also recognize the reality of our environment and keep our focus on the counter-cultural nature of our Christian calling. "The spirituality of Nazareth . . . which implies littleness, love of little things and humility, is not easy in our world. We are schooled from an early age to go up the ladder of promotion, to be outstanding, to succeed and win prizes."[15]

Unapproved: Selfish ambition

One particular type of ambition, the result of secular thinking on prestige and success penetrating the church, gets a very bad press in the New Testament because of its dire consequences. Ungodly ambition is selfish ambition. The word for ambition that occurs seven times in the New Testament always involves a fault that destroys the work of the church. This ambition, which includes no element of service, is based on self-seeking aims for personal profit and power. It's not surprising that it basically means "strife". Its effects in the Corinthian church, for example, included factions divided by which leader had baptized them; who had the best spiritual gifts; differences of opinion about eating meat offered to idols, and so on. Some of these sound like arcane matters to us today, but secular thinking on ambitions and graceless opinions can still lead us in some unwholesome directions. Have you ever listened to heated and impassioned arguments in Bible studies? Have you ever watched someone who does little in the church, rarely attends, has a high position in society, but wants to exert undue influence on church decisions? We can all think of ways in which damaging strife flows from selfish ambition. The apostles certainly had first-hand experience of this. John writes, "I wrote to the church, but Diotrephes, who loves to be first, will have nothing to do with us."[16] Paul warns in a similar vein, "Those people [the Judaizing teachers] are zealous to win you over, but for no good. What they want is to alienate you from us, so that you may be zealous for them."[17] It's amazing that these hazards emerged so early on in the spiritually prosperous atmosphere of the fledgling church. We need to be alert and ready to deal with the same sorts of problems today.

As always, James pulls no punches when he deals with such matters. He identifies the close link between ambition and bitter jealousy. Selfish ambition and heavenly wisdom do not go together. The following passage is a template for Christian living.

> Who is wise and understanding among you? Let him show it by his good life, by deeds done in the humility that comes from wisdom. But if you harbour bitter envy and selfish ambition in your hearts, do not boast about it or deny the truth. Such "wisdom" does not come down from heaven but is earthly,

unspiritual, of the devil. For where you have envy and selfish ambition, there you find disorder and every evil practice. But the wisdom that comes from heaven is first of all pure; then peace-loving, considerate, submissive, full of mercy and good fruit, impartial and sincere. Peacemakers who sow in peace raise a harvest of righteousness.[18]

Selfish ambition denies God's wise ordering of the world and is still a source of quarrels and conflicts in the church and in ministries designed to advance the kingdom. Such ambition leads us to serve ourselves rather than others such that "All actions are evaluated by their effect, positive or negative, on ourselves, rather than on promoting God's will."[19]

Try testing your motives for selfish ambition in Table 4.3. A spirit of prayer and contemplation would probably best enable you to honestly answer these six questions.

Table 4.3 Selfish ambition

1. If I achieved my most cherished ambition in life, in what ways would I bring God glory?

2. Have I compromised what I once regarded as my Christian standards to get to my present position?

3. Do I allow a spirit of competitiveness to affect my relationships with my Christian peer group?

4. When (if ever) did I last have a thorough "ambition check-up" with God?

5. Do my spiritual leaders and mentors confirm that my ambition is God-honouring rather than self-seeking? (If you haven't asked them, now would be a good time to do so.)

6. What right or wrong turnings have I made in the past with regard to my ambitions?

Selfish ambition can be crucified – and perhaps working through these questions can help you to begin to do that. We can only achieve this with complete honesty and a constant focus on Jesus as our ultimate example.

True success: Its reality and visibility

How, then, can we live according to God's measure of success in a world that views success in wholly different terms? We see the sharpness of that contrast in the life of Christ. Oswald Chambers reminds us, "Watch where Jesus went. The one dominant note in his life was to do his Father's will. His is not the way of wisdom or of success, but the way of faithfulness." Jesus captures this heavenly success criterion in a simple, but profound, statement: "I have brought you [the Father] glory on earth by completing the work you gave me to do."[20] These words give us a practical benchmark to check whether we are en route to true success. Every day we review our personal workload in terms of what we have done and what we have yet to do. But what of our "spiritual workload" – that unique set of tasks that the Master has placed in our in-tray? Many of us never quite get to them. Others of us regard these tasks as something you do when there's nothing else to do. Some of us have spent years making promises to the Lord and have never delivered on any of them. If you are a Christian in any of these categories, you are unlikely to find real success – no matter how well you stack up by the measures of the world around you. We should remember, too, that God did not design this route to success to be either boring or barren. Jesus assures us that he came "that they may have life, and have it to the full".[21] He clearly saw the obedient life as the abundant life. Do we?

True success is real, but it may not be visible – and there's the rub. How did this work out in the lives of Jesus' disciples? Simeon's biography, for example, is remarkably brief: "a man in Jerusalem . . . who was righteous and devout."[22] But he was available to do God's work when Jesus was presented in the Temple. Paul was obedient in a variety of circumstances that were far from easy, yet his focus was very evident. "I want to know Christ and the power of his resurrection and the fellowship of sharing in his sufferings, becoming like him in his death, and so, somehow, to attain to the resurrection from the dead."[23] His success measure was easily summarized. No one could say that it lacked ambition. Nor could they say that it was an easy home run. "I press on towards the goal to win the prize for which God has called me heavenwards in Christ Jesus."[24] This is the acid test – whether or not we are truly committed to "pressing on". Pleasing the Lord will lead to true success, but it may not be visible either to you or your peers. Since many Christians have a mortal dread of failure, we can only pursue this goal if we have courage and have been delivered from the many anxieties associated with the pursuit of secular success.

> The man who loves God is in an unassailable position. He has surrendered his own plans to the greater permanent plan of God, the responsibility for which is God's. He asks no favours of God but he does ask for the guiding and strength of God that, through him, God's will may be achieved. There is nothing now that can happen which cannot be turned into good for him. (J.B. Phillips)

Such words should be posted at each of life's crossroads – and especially when we are deciding what kind of ambitions to pursue.

SELAH:

> Those who have failed miserably are often the first to see God's formula for success. (Erwin Lutzer)

The essential elements of true success include a transformed mind, a consciousness of eternity, evident obedience, a spiritual appetite and humble service. Think about your attitudes and motivation. Where do these ingredients feature in your priorities?

How will you apply God's benchmarks for ambition and success to your own life?

A recent obituary for a successful businessman read as follows: "He rose from extreme poverty to great wealth – but his final ambition remained unsatisfied". In his case this ambition was recognition, and it escaped him. Pray that your burning ambition will be the right one.

---

[1] Jer. 45:5.

[2] Col. 2:8.

[3] 3 Jn. 7.

[4] Lk. 2:49,50 (NKJV).

[5] Mt. 28:18.

[6] Mt. 20:25–28.

[7] There are many sources for details on the outstanding characters in the Christian church. These include Geoffrey Hanks, *70 Great Christians* (Fearn, Ross-shire: Christian Focus Publications, 1992), from which I have drawn for this section.

[8] Rom. 1:17, quoting from Hab. 2:4.

[9] 1 Cor. 4:3,4.

[10] 2 Cor. 5:9.

[11] Rom. 15:3, quoting from Ps. 69:9.

[12] Rom. 15:20.

[13] 1 Thes. 4:11,12.

[14] Quoted in the foreword of John Johnson, *Christian Excellence: Alternative to Success* (Grand Rapids: Baker Books, 1985).

[15] Jean Vanier, *Community and Church* (New York: Paulist Press, 1989), 303.

[16] 3 Jn. 9.

[17] Gal. 4:17.

[18] Jas. 3:13–18.

[19] Robert Schnase, *Ambition in Ministry: Our Spiritual Struggle with Success and Competition* (Nashville, TN: Abingdon Press, 1993), 44.

[20] Jn. 17:4.

[21] Jn. 10:10.

[22] Lk. 2:25.

[23] Phil. 3:10,11, and see 2 Cor. 6:3–11 for a summary of his trials.

[24] Phil. 3:14.

5

Do Not Be Misled by the Praise of Others

"They remembered that God was their Rock, that God Most High was their Redeemer. But then they would flatter him with their mouths, lying to him with their tongues". (Ps. 78:35,36)

Outline

The praise that we receive from other people exerts influence on our lives in subtle ways. Because we find praise of any kind so pleasing, we often discount its long-term, life-shaping, potential.

Problem? What problem?: How do we handle praise from others? And how does God see it influencing our lives?

Minds that are responsive – but to what?: What does it really mean to surrender our thought processes to God? What are the different ways that praise from others reaches us?

Case studies: Reacting to the praise of others: Three contemporary, real-life case studies on patronage, success and adulation show us how the long-term effects of praise can bring people to crossroads experiences.

Pride and flattery: How do you know when pride and flattery have stunted your effectiveness for God?

Problem? What problem?

We all need praise, but not all of us can handle it – that's the problem. Some might say, "That's ridiculous. We're not fools. Everyone can distinguish between praise that is for our good and that which is designed to deceive and mislead." Or, "I know lots of people who are swayed by the praise of others – but that's because they're vulnerable and insecure. They need lots of positive reinforcement. But I'm not like that. I'm comfortable with who I am, so this isn't a problem for me." Or, "I was once misled by the praise of a boss who grossly exaggerated my prospects and then fired me. But I've learned from that experience, and it will never happen again." These responses are representative of the prevailing idea that this is only a problem for the few or a lesson that we learn and then move on. This is not the biblical view. Indeed, this is a root and branch problem to which all Christians at all times are susceptible. For example, consider these two proverbs. "The crucible for silver and the furnace for gold, but man is tested by the praise he receives."[1] This is consistent with other biblical teaching, as we will see below, and strongly suggests that God regards the "praise of men" as that which tests the disciples' character – in the same way as the crucible and furnace have long been identified with silver and gold. If that's God's expectation, we cannot lightly shrug off this subject. We may not, of course, be tested to destruction by the praise of others. This praise may even prove to be a force for beneficial change that is to God's glory. The second proverb considers the obligations that praise sometimes creates – not all of which may be healthy. "Many curry favour with a ruler, and everyone is the friend of a man who gives gifts."[2] We will look at the perils of patronage later in this chapter.

This question of praise is a serious matter in God's eyes, and we need to understand its good and bad aspects. It is a basic human need, for people of all ages and stages, to receive praise and encouragement. Most of us do not give enough praise, and some of us feel that we do not receive enough of it. Praise stimulates us to be more confident, to put in greater effort and it helps to motivate us. The most helpful kind of praise often comes by degrees – to distinguish between indifferent, good and excellent performance. We can all benefit from informal praise in the small things of everyday life, as well as from a more formal and reflective review of how we are handling a job or a project over the longer term. It is fascinating to see how different national and organizational cultures treat praise and rewards. In several countries I have observed the habit of covering the walls of homes with vast numbers of certificates and awards. These can range from the amusing to the bizarre – from an ancient driving certificate to the birthday of the family parrot and fourth place in the breaststroke at a long-forgotten school swimming gala. Many an executive wall, too, is similarly festooned with awards given to the organization and the individual. I have no problem with this and indeed have encouraged it in many different organizations – including Christian ones.

Where, then, does the "praise of men" fit into this? In considering the negative side of praise we have to look at the motivation of the one who is giving the praise as well as at the state of mind of the one receiving the praise. Why it is said, and how it is heard, are both critical. The motives of the giver may well be pure, a genuine recognition of achievement. On the other hand, motives may simply be neutral with no intent to deceive or misinform, but the giver of praise may nevertheless lead us to make decisions, go in directions, or develop characteristics that are not honouring God. Such praise may come from many different sources – from those with whom we live, work or socialize. This praise can boost our egos in undesirable ways, blind us to God's instructions, deceive us, reduce our dependence on God, weaken our faith and feed hypocrisy. The Bible makes special mention of some damaging reactions to the "praise of men", including pride and the effects of flattery, which we will consider below.

Minds that are responsive – but to what?

Before we are able to respond to these challenges, we need to look more closely at the state of our minds as Christians. The extent to which Jesus is the Lord of our minds will determine our response to the "praise of men". None of us can claim to have the fullness of the mind of Christ. We simply don't always think like Christians. John Stott says that "One of the highest and noblest functions of man's mind is to listen to God's Word and so to read his mind and think his thoughts." Paul gives us insight into how that is possible

> For though we live in the world, we do not wage war as the world does. The weapons we fight with are not the weapons of the world. On the contrary, they have divine power to demolish strongholds. We demolish arguments and every pretension that sets itself up against the knowledge of God, and we take captive every thought to make it obedient to Christ.[3]

The process is clear: we filter the praise of others by taking each thought that is triggered captive – thereby making "it obedient to Christ" (as it must be in order to please him). But we have to be willing to spend the time and expend the necessary intellectual effort to do this.

The following three examples put flesh on this principle. A wife says to her husband: "Darling, you are a marvellous preacher and a wonderful communicator. This is your true calling." Unfortunately, none of his church leaders and no one who hears him preaching shares this view. Even when such praise comes from his wife, the husband needs to check this seed of doubt that has been sown in his mind with others, and he needs to prayerfully consider whether this is God's call or not. A social contact tells a respected Christian friend: "Joe, you are wasted in your present job. You are a brilliant leader and what you are doing makes poor use of all your talents. Come and work with me and we'll get rich together." This form of praise presses the sensitive button of Joe's stewardship of his gifts – something he's been anxious about. It also offers the carrot of greater rewards, but this invitation does not specify the costs of achieving them. At the very least, Joe needs to seriously consider how God is using him in his present job and whether or not he could use his gifts there in other ways, what these financial rewards really would be (and at what cost) and whether that is something he feels strongly about pursuing, and what his motivations would be for accepting this offer. Only then will he be able to begin to discern the way of obedience. Bill works from a London base for a multinational company that regards its senior executives as totally mobile. After his annual review his boss tells him: "Bill, you're a class act and I've given you the highest possible performance rating again this year. You're ready for a radical change – in terms of geography and function. We want you to move from your role as financial controller to head up human resources for the US, based in Chicago. By the way, the executive board has approved this promotion, so it would not be a good idea to turn it down." Bill would, of course, have to discuss this praise-based ultimatum with his family first. But as a Christian he also needs confirmation from the Lord to make such a move. Being a "company man" by repute, he may struggle to give enough attention to the latter part of the process. Many Christians struggle simply because they don't like the Lord's answers. Bill is at a crossroads.

In the passage from 2 Corinthians above, Paul uses a lot of military imagery. The war against ideas, philosophies and general ways of thinking is not easy. And the praise of others is invariably pleasing to our ears. Paul lived in an environment where "stir-fry" Christian practice was popular – people would bring any bundle of ideas, competing worldviews and mix of deities together and brand it "Christian". Paul would have none of it, and neither would God – then or now. Hence the demanding standard is to bring *every* thought captive – including those placed in our minds by others. The choice at its simplest and sharpest is this: we either hear the praise of others amid the multiple philosophies of Mars Hill, where anything goes, or we receive and then distil that praise in the shadow of Calvary's hill. We all need to be vigilant about the impressions that the praise of others make upon us. "A simple man believes anything, but a prudent man gives thought to his steps."[4]

REFLECTION:

Do you need to take more time to bring every thought captive in obedience to Christ? These thoughts may or may not be related to the praise of others – there are many other moral and spiritual issues that require the same discipline. Be encouraged by this assurance in our warfare: "His divine power has given us everything we need for life and godliness through our knowledge of him who called us by his own glory and goodness."[5]

CASE STUDIES:
Reacting to the praise of others

The following case studies look at a variety of reactions to the praise of others. Each case study portrays incidents that have brought the main character to a major crossroads decision. In the twelfth century, Bernard of Clairvaux wrote: "It is no great thing to be humble when you are brought low; but to be humble when you are praised is a great and rare attainment." Clearly, this is not a new problem for Christians.

Vernon – entrapped by patronage: Vernon was the managing director of a small, highly successful specialist engineering company called Sailing Solutions that made and installed navigation equipment for yachts. The company was owned by John Marsh, an entrepreneur with diverse business interests (not all of which were known to Vernon). His business model was to invest in smaller companies and find good people to run them. Vernon had joined the company as an electronics apprentice and progressed to his post over a period of 20 years. John had the highest regard for Vernon – for his hard work, business performance and the integrity he showed in all his dealings. John would say to some of his business associates, "I may be a bit of a rogue at times, but with men like Vernon around I present a good face to the world. It's not for me, but I can live with his Christian principles so long as they don't get in the way of making profits." John's plan for Vernon was to pay him so much in salary and bonuses that he wouldn't move to an equivalent post elsewhere in the district – and John knew that he wanted to stay in the geographical area. Vernon understood John's motivation, and he went along with it for several years. Then he began to worry about the effect this patronage was having on his life. John was demanding, but normally within reasonable bounds. But things started to change in several directions. John began to gamble and incur heavy losses, and this in turn led to cash flow problems which began, over a period of two years, to impact the amount of money he had available to support Vernon's business. John had always been detached from the daily business of Sailing Solutions, but now he became very intrusive and, for the first time, Vernon saw that John's business ethics were questionable. Sensing that Vernon was uncomfortable, however, John heaped more praise on him and offered to double his salary to head off any question of him leaving the company. John needed him more than ever, and he began to blackmail him by telling him how many jobs would be lost if he was not running the business. Alarm bells were now ringing in Vernon's head. He knew that he badly needed to take time out and work through whether these fine words had taken him to the edge of obedience to the Lord – whether these thoughts had been "taken captive" as he knew they should. When he stopped to think, he realized it had been almost ten years since he had asked the Lord about this – after a men's retreat he had attended called "The Christian at Work". He knew now that he had been unwittingly entrapped by the praise of a very persuasive man.

Frank – seduced by success: Frank was a great preacher and an outstanding theology student. A suburban church that was declining invited him to become their pastor, in the hope that his energy and vision would transform its prospects. The church buildings were in poor condition, and the congregation ageing. Some godly elders influenced his decision to take up the challenge. He respected what they had achieved in the past, and they accepted that things had to change. Predictably, the nature and pace of change became an issue sooner rather than later. By the end of his first six months in the church, Frank had a blueprint for reform to present to the elders and church council. His plan covered the music and teaching programmes, the church buildings and a radical new stewardship programme. Frank had gone for the "surprise them with a blockbuster" approach, based on minimum consultation with anyone, including his senior elders. Not surprisingly, his plan met with a lot of resistance, both at the meeting and over the ensuing six months. Frank was frustrated, but he had a daring (and dangerous) plan. The root problem was a lack of support from the leadership, so he set out to change it. He had identified a number of experienced business and professional men in his area that he had met socially at dinners, playing golf and at the sports club. They all thought he was great and a "breath of fresh air" for a pastor. One or two of them did attend his church on a casual basis, and several others were on the edge of Christian life. "I could really change things with this team as my leadership – they have energy and the perfect skills match of architecture, building, finance and project management. They don't know a lot about theology and pastoral skills, but others will cover these gaps. And they are my men, who solidly support me." So he set out with that mission and formed a change team with his new friends, having persuaded them all to become church members. He bulldozed his way past his elders, several of whom left the church or judiciously retired. The church council were browbeaten into going with the original change programme. But there was a price to pay. Dave, the spokesman for his new change team, had a word with Frank. "We need numbers, so we think that you should revamp your whole approach to church. It's too traditional, the sermons are too long and too hard-hitting. Lighten up a bit, and let's get the marketing going – we have great potential here." Although there was little spiritual content in what Dave was saying, since he wrapped his proposal up in honeyed words Frank bought into it all. The numbers attending the church doubled within months, and a new building programme was planned that would involve a large new site at the edge of town and four times as much space. Frank was thrilled – his dream was being realized. It was not without some tensions – but that was church life, and his team was experienced and robust. Things went along for another two years. The congregation was now five times larger than it was when he first came. At an anniversary weekend to celebrate his fifth year of ministry, three of his closest college colleagues visited the church as invited guests. They were shocked to see how much of his spiritual vision Frank had lost. They saw that his sermons were crowd pleasing, but little else. Saddened and stunned, they sat down with Frank over supper. "Who have you been listening to for these past few years, Frank? You seem to be running a content-free church to maximize numbers." Frank was deeply offended and very defensive. But his conscience was pricked. He did not want to admit that he had given more attention to the praise of others than to the approval of God.[6] And now he had a major choice to make – but was it too late?

Madge – diverted by adulation: Madge Johnston had always had a natural gift for singing. Her gift was fostered in church and formally developed by high-quality voice training at school and college. Her range and tone as a soprano were widely acclaimed by audiences and skilled teachers alike. As her schedule became increasingly demanding, she seemed capable of rising to every occasion. By her late teens she had appeared on both radio and television – initially in Christian programmes, but increasingly on shows designed to spot and promote young talent. She was working closely with a number of Christian bands and worship groups and had recorded solo parts on discs that had been well received. Madge realized that she faced two dilemmas. First she had to decide whether music would be her career. And second, if she made that choice, how would she mix the spiritual and the secular? She liked the idea of "crossover" work, or maintaining a dual presence in these two arenas, but she knew that this might be a hazardous journey. Although she was of a different generation, she admired people like Sir Cliff Richard in this regard. Unfortunately her parents did not share her Christian vision and were very ambitious for Madge – pushing her into every opportunity. Her father became her manager, and this produced its own tensions. "Did you see these reviews from the rock concert? They're fabulous! The audience loved you. We must follow up on the offers for the European tour and the recording contract. You can do the Christian stuff in your spare time – but it just doesn't have the same potential." By age twenty, Madge had fallen in love with the adulation of her many fans and no longer did any Christian singing – except during her rare visits to church in distant cities. One night after an exhausting concert schedule in Berlin, she switched on the God Channel on the hotel TV. It was a worship gathering from Australia led by Hillsongs, and it reminded her of what she had turned her back on, and of the sense of "calling" that she had walked away from. She knew that the "praise of men" had shaped her choices – but these were now written in contracts and formal agreements that were very difficult to change. She felt a deep and lasting conviction over the next three weeks. She had to have some difficult conversations with her earthly father, having heard so clearly once again from her heavenly Father.

REFLECTION:

These are not easy situations. Over time, praise from others can have enduring, transforming and life-shaping effects, diverting our attention from the purposes of God. What you would do if you found yourself in similar circumstances to Frank, John and Madge? Decisions like this require time and thought to explore all the possible ramifications. Real life is rather like that.

Pride and flattery

The Bible gives a lot of attention to some of the nastier behavioural consequences of listening to the "praise of men". Here we will focus on two of them: pride and flattery.

Pride: Pride develops in Christians for many reasons, and praise is only one of its sources – but, as we have seen, it is one that we easily underestimate. Rather like a disease, pride strikes the young, old, rich and poor alike. If we harbour pride in our hearts, it is usually evident in our lives and behaviour. Benjamin Franklin once wrote of pride, "Even if I could conceive that I had completely overcome it, I should probably be proud of my humility." Let's look at some of the aspects of pride that can be fuelled by the praise of others.

The Bible teaches that all pride is a sin against God's sovereignty. "In his pride the wicked does not seek him; in all his thoughts there is no room for God."[7] "Blessed is the man who makes the LORD his trust, who does not look to the proud, to those who turn aside to false gods."[8] "For everything in the world – the cravings of sinful man, the lust of his eyes and the boasting of what he has and does – comes not from the Father but from the world."[9] Praise can generate a pride in our hearts that causes us to listen less to God and more to other people. When we are not paying attention to God, we offer him little or no chance to shape our lives. As Augustine said, "It was pride that changed angels into devils; it is humility that makes men into angels."

The Bible gives many examples of pride sapping people's attention away from God's sovereign power. Most of these people, including Uzziah and Belshazzar, develop this pride based on the praise of others. "But after Uzziah became powerful, his pride led to his downfall. He was unfaithful to the LORD his God, and entered the temple of the LORD to burn incense on the altar of incense."[10] And Daniel confronted Belshazzar with the following words: ". . . You praised the gods of silver and gold, of bronze, iron, wood and stone, which cannot see or hear or understand. But you did not honour the God who holds in his hand your life and all your ways."[11] Both of these men have been corrupted. They have listened to others, worshipped God-substitutes and failed to fulfil their God-given mandates. Alan Redpath was right when he observed that pride is the route to something much more sinister. "Pride is the idolatrous worship of ourselves, and that is the national religion of hell."

How can I tell if I am proud? Truthfully answering the seven questions in Table 5.1 will give you some clues.

Table 5.1 Am I proud?

- How do I respond to advice and criticism?
- Do I ever apologize and admit to being wrong?
- Do I hate proud people – without realizing that I am just like them?
- Do I enjoy boasting?
- Have I ever asked God to deliver me from pride?
- Am I sensitive to others, making a conscious effort not to be vain or overbearing?
- Do I think that my own opinions are inviolate?

2. *Flattery:* Most of us are susceptible to flattery at one time or another – even when we see it for what it is. I know from my own experience (see, for example, the incidents recounted in Chapter 1) that flattery is often the most dangerous aspect of the "praise of man". The Bible describes flattery with harsh words. For example, "May the LORD cut off all flattering lips and every boastful tongue"[12] and "Whoever says to the guilty, 'You are innocent' – peoples will curse him and nations denounce him."[13] These verses don't leave open the possibility that flattery is innocent or an innocuous game for which everyone knows the rules. Jesus saw right through such duplicity. "So the spies [from the teachers of the law and the high priests] questioned him: 'Teacher, we know that you speak and teach what is right, and that you do not show partiality but teach the way of God in accordance with the truth.'"[14] These flattering words were spoken to elicit a response from Jesus that would incriminate him and divert him from his task. Most flattery is based on hyperbole, a method of exaggeration that appeals to many because it contains a grain of truth. We need to be on our guard, remembering that flattery is the breeding ground of pride and self-deceit – both of which are enemies of God's rule in our lives.

C.S. Lewis described the ubiquitous nature of pride and its damaging effects in no uncertain terms

> There is an evil of which no man in the world is free: which everyone in the world loathes when he sees it in someone else; and of which hardly any people, except Christians, ever imagine that they are guilty themselves . . . The essential vice, the utmost evil, is pride . . . Pride leads to every other vice; it is the complete anti-God state of mind.

SELAH:

What are your current struggles with the praise of others? (Look carefully at the whole range of human influences in your life – the truly influential ones are often easy to miss.)

Have you yourself praised others in the past in a way that was damaging? What are your temptations in this area in terms of wanting to be liked and accepted or wanting to control and influence others?

What is God's key message for you from this chapter? And what do you plan to do about it?

---

[1] Prov. 27:21.
[2] Prov. 19:6.
[3] 2 Cor. 10:3–5.
[4] Prov. 14:15.
[5] 2 Pet. 1:3.
[6] This case study was inspired by the novel *And the Shofar Blew* by Francine Rivers (Wheaton, IL: Tyndale, 2003).
[7] Ps. 10:4.
[8] Ps. 40:4.
[9] 1 Jn. 2:16.
[10] 2 Chr. 26:16.
[11] Dan. 5:23.
[12] Ps. 12:3.
[13] Prov. 24:24.
[14] Lk. 20:21.

6

Test and See if You Have a Servant's Heart

"Send forth your light and your truth, let them guide me; let them bring me to your holy mountain, to the place where you dwell."
(Ps. 43:3)

Outline

Unselfish living among Christians is relatively rare, but it is part of our calling as Christ's followers to serve others.

Service at the crossroads: What is God's definition of service? How can crossroads experiences transform our servant hearts?

Service with a difference: What is distinctive about the content, quality and obligation of Christian service? Are we motivated to serve by love, gratitude, eternity, rewards or fear?

A few lessons from experience: What does this teaching about service look like in real life?

Service at the crossroads

Every Christian is, by definition, a servant – but not every Christian has a servant's heart. The first thought of the person with a servant's heart is the service of the Lord. The nature of our heart is revealed when we are tested, when we face crossroads experiences. Jesus clearly defined Christian service with these words: "The man who loves his life will lose it, while the man who hates his life in this world will keep it for eternal life. Whoever serves me must follow me; and where I am, my servant also will be."[1] This definition is our yardstick. The servant is a devoted follower – spiritually, mentally, attitudinally and geographically close to where the Master wants him or her to be. "Loving life" here implies living in a self-centred and selfish manner for our own benefit. Those who love their own lives often despise the lives of others, abusing and manipulating them for their own ends. Encouraging people to "hate life" does not mean that we should have low self-esteem or be negative about God's gifts or his plans. Rather, those with this attitude to life choose to live for the blessing and benefit of others. Such people understand how this life fits into the next. They recognize the difference between bringing glory to themselves and glorifying God. They see servanthood in terms of wise stewardship of God's gifts and as an honour to their Master. In short, they have servant hearts. "Do I have a heart like this?" is the question that each one of us needs to ask. As Victor Nyquist said, "You do not do God a favour by serving him. He honours you by allowing you to serve him".

Psalm 43:3 helps us to gauge all aspects of our response as disciples, including our service. Although as Christians we acknowledge our source of "light and truth", we are not always willing to be guided by these precepts. As a result, we are rarely at the holy mountain or in touch with where God wants us to be.

> God the Father, Son and Holy Ghost isn't a consulting firm we bring in to give us expert advice on how to run our lives. The gospel life isn't something we learn about and then put together with instructions from the manufacturer: it is something we become as God does his work of creation and salvation in us

and as we accustom ourselves to a life of belief and obedience and prayer. (Eugene Peterson)

Are we allowing God to do his work in developing our servant hearts?

I know several Christians who have lost their hearts for service somewhere along the pathways of life. I also know many who have found (or rediscovered) their servant hearts as a result of crossroads experiences. As you are introduced to a few of these people here, note the basic changes in their circumstances that were the drivers for change.

Martin gradually lost his servant heart in the five years after he married a Christian who did not share his enthusiasm for the Lord. They looked so compatible on paper, but time proved otherwise. His wife did not support his continued involvement in youth ministries in their area. She simply "loved life" too much and was not willing to accommodate the needs of others. In the interests of domestic harmony, Martin never bothered to find another area of service. For the moment at least, a talent has been buried.

Wilson lost his servant heart 20 years ago. He still blames this on the fact that close Christian friends let him down on a big church project. There was a violent and protracted disagreement about money, and this destroyed both his friendships and his witness. He has never forgiven these friends and carries a grudge about what they have done to his life. Since then he has been lost to the Christian arts ministries in which he once excelled. He rarely attends church.

Elizabeth lost her servant heart as result of a church schism. Major theological arguments among church leaders ultimately led to the formation of three separate churches in her town. Devastated by the hypocrisy and lack of grace demonstrated during these events, she withdrew from her involvement in the church pre-school programme that she loved. It has been ten years since she left her church, and she has never found another one.

Gerald faced the devastating prospect of losing his job, as a result of a major budgetary review, after an outstanding career in government service. He had a year or so to consider his options before his department was closed, during which he became aware of God's call to use his skills in a new way. He rediscovered a servant heart that he had nearly lost through the pressures of his career. He is now using his experience in a new way, as a highly effective administrator in several Christian charities.

Lorna found fresh scope for her servant heart in a new caring ministry. Her church asked for a team of people to commit their professional skills to helping low-income families plan their financial affairs. Time pressures in her accounting practice had restricted her availability, but a sermon on stewardship challenged her deeply. She negotiated a part-time contract with her partners, became a true tent-maker and threw herself into this rewarding work for which she displayed a real aptitude.

Tony was moved by his company three years ago to a new area several hundred miles away. He was busy with his new job and found it difficult to connect with a new Christian community – although he did try and finally succeeded. Everything seemed highly organized in this large, welcoming church and he could see little need for his specialist computing skills. But he had a servant heart and was responsive to God's call. Today he runs an IT advisory service for several Christian ministries and has never felt more fulfilled.

REFLECTION:

> Too many are willing to sit at God's table, but not to work in his field. (Vance Havner)

> God forces no one, for love cannot compel, and God's service is a thing of perfect freedom. (Hans Denk)

Many of us struggle with the inextricable Christian concepts of obligation and freedom. What is your attitude to Christian service? Would you say that you have a true "servant heart"?

Are you at a crossroads at which you need to consider (or reconsider) Christian service?

Service with a difference

We usually think of the word "service" in our role as consumers. We are either delighted or disgusted by the service we receive at the supermarket, garage, bank or airline or from a tradesman, tour operator, government institution and so on. We assess various service providers based on a published standard of service, a verbal promise, a promise made by publicity or an expectation based on the service provision of competitors. As Christians, we have made similar promises about our service – albeit on a higher plane and before the Lord. But simply by professing our faith we have declared our standards, raised expectations and made promises to those who interact with us in this world. Our peers may not be "consumers", but they are observers. And we would like them to become "consumers" of the gospel of grace.

Having made this link to our consumer society, however, we also acknowledge that Christian service is distinctive in terms of its content, quality and obligations. We will look at these three elements in turn. First its content. What is the nature of this service we are called to? The New Testament word for service is the one from which we derive the English word "liturgy". The Greek word referred to the service a priest gave in the temple of a god but Paul used it, for example, to refer to serving others, as in the collection for the poor Christians in Jerusalem. "This service that you perform is not only supplying the needs of God's people but is also overflowing in many expressions of thanks to God."[2] The word was also used in the New Testament to refer to religious service, as in the words of the Holy Spirit, "Set apart for me Barnabas and Saul for the work to which I have called them".[3] The word's later usage was both more mundane and inclusive, in that it came to simply mean a "workman". William Barclay captures the essence of the word, "The Christian is a man who works for God and men, first, because he desires to, with his whole heart, and second, because he is compelled to, because the love of Christ constrains him."[4] It is not surprising, therefore, that the following verse occurs in a passage about being made alive in Christ. It shows how that new life is inextricably connected to a servant heart. "For we are God's workmanship, created in Christ Jesus to do good works, which God prepared in advance for us to do."[5] It is important and exciting to realize that God may well have prepared specific things for each of us to do beyond our present crossroads. As one who has spent most of his professional life as a strategic planner in the world of business, I have to say I'm glad that God is in control of strategic planning for our lives.

Another distinctive of Christian service is its quality. It's possible that many of us engaged in different kinds of Christian service will acknowledge failure as we read these next few paragraphs, in which case we will need to repent and pray. A person with a genuine servant's heart:

Does not demand recognition: This is perhaps the most counter-cultural challenge for our generation. So much of public Christian service is predicated upon recognition – even if we neither demand nor seek it. There is a fine balance between recognizing a person's gifting and giving them encouragement – and fuelling a demand for recognition. This requires wisdom beyond our own. In giving to ministries and churches, for example, Christians increasingly want public recognition. This desire disregards clear biblical instruction. "Freely you have received, freely give."[6] We must guard against this.

Does not demand reward: The Christian servant knows that there will be an eternal reward, but he or she has to accept that there may be little or no temporal reward. If we are honest, we have to admit that this is hard to swallow at times. God has committed to provide for us as we serve in his name. Humbly and gratefully accepting his provision is a far cry from demanding (or expecting) a reward. Paul reminded Christian slaves – the most disenfranchised people in his society – that "Whatever you do, work at it with all your heart, as working for the Lord, not for men, since you know that you will receive an inheritance from the Lord as a reward. It is the Lord Christ you are serving."[7]

Does not demand rights: This is another difficult issue. Our service has to implement the all-pervading principle of love, and that does involve deferring to others. "Honour one another above yourselves. Never be lacking in zeal, but keep your spiritual fervour, serving the Lord."[8] In sharp contrast, the Bible gives many examples of people feigning to serve the Lord without a servant's heart – who end up instead pursuing power, financial rewards or pre-eminence. While many of us will not end up at these extremes, we do need to keep in mind that all aspects of service demand a combination of leadership and love. So whereas a servant with a servant's heart does not insist on getting his own way, he may well need to deal with situations in which his way is best, even though others may disagree. This falls short of demanding rights, but in a pastoral context it may be seen as such. We also need to be careful not to become so busy in Christ's service that we forget to love him. In all of our service, we need to pray for God's grace and strength and wisdom.

And what of the obligations of Christian service? Rick Warren says that "a 'non-serving Christian' is a contradiction in terms".[9] While choosing my words with some care, I defy you to read the following verse and come to any other conclusion. "But you are a chosen people, a royal priesthood, a holy nation, a people belonging to God, that you may declare the praises of him who called you out of darkness into his wonderful light."[10] Using any one of the great variety of gifts that God has given to the church will enable us to serve in a way that "declares his praises". There are also many hindrances to service, however – we noted only a few of them in the case studies above. We can place limitations on our service, for example, as Moses did with his assessment of his communication and leadership qualities, or as Jonah tried to do with God's choice of a venue for his service. Many of us are willing to serve God, but only at our convenience or provided we can serve people we like. Attitudinal barriers include laziness and ingratitude, to say nothing of pride and self-centredness. But in all of this we need to remember that being a servant of God is a great honour, and the obligation to serve comes laden with opportunities, satisfaction and joy. Nor

should we fail to observe that many of the biblical servants did not have problem-free lives. We are inclined to dwell at times on the uniqueness of twenty-first century living, with all its complexities. But Paul had poor health, Thomas doubted, Peter denied, Moses was both old and reluctant and Jeremiah was suicidal at times. The Lord can take us, wherever we are, and develop a servant heart in us – but we have to be willing.

> Give me the lowest place: not that I dare
> Ask for that lowest place, but Thou hast died
> That I might love and share
> Thy glory by Thy side
> Give me the lowest place: or if for me
> That lowest place too high, make one more low
> Where I may sit and see
> My God and love Thee so. (Christina Rossetti)

What is our motivation for cultivating a servant heart? The New Testament identifies at least five major factors, as well as another that we will put in a slightly different category. Table 6.1 sets out these five in what might be a reasonable order of priority (with some overlap).

Table 6.1 Motivations for Christian Service

Love: This is first a love for God and then, from that, a love for all others. We show that love through obedience; a desire to please God and bring him glory; a commitment to work for the benefit of God's kingdom; and an aspiration to know him and discover his purposes for our lives.

Gratitude: Service is a response to God's gracious actions on our behalf; it is a form of thanksgiving and worship. In the light of his blessings we are called to live for him, serve him with thanksgiving and offer our bodies as a sacrifice to him.

Eternity: Earthly service can be, and probably should be, motivated by our preparation for service in the coming kingdom. We are to be faithful in our current responsibilities and endure suffering to this end. The letter to the Hebrews, in particular, lays out many promises regarding the share that the faithful will have in Christ's future rule.

Rewards: Our service can be motivated by the rewards that God gives in this life, as well as by those he promises in eternity. There is much biblical emphasis on the judgement seat of Christ as the forum for future rewards for the Christian. The Lord assumes that all Christians are accountable (as shown graphically in many of the parables), and treasures and crowns are on offer to the faithful.[11] The Christian community as a whole does not have a well-developed understanding of losing out on heavenly rewards. As we saw above, however, we have to examine our motives carefully and be sure that rewards are not a selfish motivation. Service that is based in selfish motivation will bring no glory to God and no credit to the Christian community.

Duty: Some Christians rightly see service as a direct consequence of choosing to follow the Lord. Jesus himself did what God had called him to do in securing our redemption, but he did it willingly. So, too, Paul wanted to live up to the "high calling" that God gave him. This is where stewardship comes in for all of us, as we are asked to deploy God-given resources in a faithful way. The same applies to the service that is our witness as we are faithful stewards of the gospel message.

I did not include fear as one of our motivations for service in Table 6.1 because I regard it as an inferior motivation – especially when it is compared to love. You may disagree. I do think, however, that fear can be an important part of the process of developing a servant heart for some Christians in certain states of mind. Christians may fear the judgement seat, shame or loss of reward, or even that they will face judgement while here on earth. There is a more positive link between fear and reverence, and it is certain that more of us would have servant hearts if we truly understood the holiness of God.

REFLECTION:

> What you are is God's gift to you; what you do with yourself is your gift to God. (Danish proverb)

If you struggle with desiring recognition, rewards or rights for your own service, how will you correct this? How would you rank your motivations for service (from Table 6.1)? If you lack motivation for service, take some time to reflect on which motivation from Table 6.1 moves you most. Reflect on your service over the time since you became a Christian. Would you say that your servant heart is maturing or in a state of atrophy? If the latter, what steps will you take to develop your service for Christ?

A few lessons from experience

As you reflect on your own service – past, present and future – you might find the following few lessons that I have learned along the way to be helpful. I will confess before I begin that I have always wrestled with busyness, in both my professional and church life.

Mentors: Various mentors have helped me in many ways over the years – from my early student days, when wise mentors helped me to establish a pattern of Christian service that I could manage alongside my academic commitments. This guidance

taught me to focus – perhaps more narrowly than I would have liked. During those years I helped with Sunday services in a senior citizens' home before my own church services and also helped to lead a para-church ministry for young Christians on Sunday evenings. It was good advice to focus, although I would have liked to have been able to be more involved in my university Christian Union. In more recent years, other mentors have played a different and more strategic role in my life. I understand focus and am very strict about not adding my name to board listings of Christian ministries that I will not have the time to really help – so in addition to my own church eldership and lay preaching commitments in various churches, I take direct responsibility in only a few other ministries where I feel that I have the time and skills to help. Mentors have aided me considerably in defining what these ministries should be. From time to time over the years I have contemplated full-time ministry. The consistent advice from those I trust and respect was to stay where I was, be open to God using me in my diverse public and professional posts, and progressively mobilize that business experience for the kingdom. That is what I have done in adopting the tent-making approach to a portfolio career that I mentioned in Chapter 1, and it was wise counsel. If you do not have a mentor, find one soon who can give you honest and fearless advice with grace and love – and Paul is not available!

Gifts: J.E. O'Day outlines an excellent approach to identifying our gifts.[12] He suggests five steps: pray daily to ask God to reveal your gifts; study the Bible passages on spiritual gifts; contemplate your desires, joys and inclinations; seek affirmation from mature and wise Christians as to what your gifts might be; and experiment by putting your "suspected gifts" into practice. While this is a very personal process, mentors can also help here. I benefited from biblical teaching on gifts in my early years and was specifically encouraged to experiment with communicating and administration. Others saw these gifts in me long before I did, and their advice gave me ample opportunities to experiment. I am grateful to God that I have also been able to use my professional skills in Christian service. I have observed many others who were not able (or willing) to use their skills in Christian activities and so have failed to see how God has shaped them for service. Many people who rigidly separate work and faith do not make that link. As a young lecturer, for example, I found the challenge of teaching economics to large groups of engineers who had no interest in the subject prepared me well for winning audiences in Christian settings – especially rowdy young people. I firmly believe that we should never stop asking God to reveal our gifts to us. We may not see any radical changes, but there are many new experiences and some new skill sets that we forget to log and whose relevance we can fail to see. One of my skills in that category might sound odd to you. Having chaired business meetings of all kinds for many years, I can now do this reasonably well – and I have found that it is a key requirement in many Christian contexts for the effective running of these organizations. Ask God's advice about how you can use your gifts –he has given them to you for a purpose. Your gift may be scarce, one that God urgently needs you to use, and you don't know about it.

Motivation: Although I have been motivated to serve since my teenage years, I would not claim to have had a true servant heart all that time. Like so many busy professionals, I did not always balance my priorities well, and sometimes I did the work I wanted to do rather than what God might have preferred that I do. For example, at times I took on too many preaching engagements and the two to three nights per week I spent in preparation was time away from my wife and family. My motivations for service have been primarily love and duty. I have a strong sense that I committed to follow Christ, and follow I must. But there have been times when I have not listened enough to his agenda. For example, I recall a conversation when I was in my early thirties with a Christian friend who was asking when I would become a professor. I explained to him, and to others, that this was very unlikely since my Christian interests took so much of my time. I had never played at common room politics, nor had I devoted enough time to career aggrandizement as such. Within 18 months I was invited to take up a chair that I subsequently held for 24 years. So much for my understanding of God's ways. This move was significant in positioning me for Christian witness in my community and beyond. In short, the Lord took my motivation to succeed and used it for his purposes.

Stewardship and change: I mentioned earlier that we should never stop asking for God's wisdom on how we should use his resources. When we do ask, and really mean it, he sometimes surprises us. So it was that in the summer of 2001, after sensing for almost twenty years that I should use the skills I had developed in professional academic writing in service to the Lord, he finally got through to me. I was invited to do a seminar at the Keswick Convention that year, and "Whose life is it anyway?" was the topic I chose. I wanted to use this as a vehicle to explore busyness, stewardship, success, ambition and a host of related topics. Following discussion with several inquirers after the seminar, I had a burning conviction that I needed to write on this topic and reach a much wider audience. They were all issues that I knew about and had struggled with personally. The Lord continued to prompt me over the coming weeks, but by then I was totally convicted that this book had to be written over the next four months. I have rarely been so burdened. The initial book grew into a trilogy, dealing with the related topics of work and money. But this experience brought me to a crossroads. The Lord gave me the strength of conviction necessary to quickly solve it. I felt a moral dilemma about continuing to hold a senior academic post when it was improbable that I would continue to be as active in academic publishing. My vice-chancellor encouraged me to continue as I was, but understood (and respected) my dilemma and left the decision to me. I resigned my post in summer 2003 in order to redeploy the writing part of my life for the Lord. This was the right decision, I did not do it lightly, and I know that God has honoured it. Should I have done this earlier? Probably not. I now see that the skills and experience that I was accumulating over the years are invaluable and allow me to speak with credibility to audiences that I could never have reached 20 years ago. The Lord is wise and patient, but when the call finally comes we need to listen. Have you had a similar call but have yet to respond?

I must confess to having a deep concern about inconsistency in Christian service. Many people seem content to have flushes of enthusiasm that stir them into action for brief periods, with years of inaction and indecision in between. While active, they lament that others do not share their passion and vision. While inactive, they are cynical, critical and destructive. We need to pray for an end to this waste of God's resources wherever we find it and encourage others to develop true servant hearts. As the Lord said to the church in Laodicea, "I know your deeds, that you are neither cold nor hot. I wish you were either one or the other!"[13]

> There is no coldness, Lord, in Thee
> O keep us kindled, lest we bring
> To our dear Lord of Calvary
> Dead ashes as our offering. (Amy Carmichael)

SELAH:

> I am only one,
> But still I am one.
> I cannot do everything,
> But still I can do something;
> And because I cannot do everything
> I will not refuse to do the something that I can do. (Edward Everett Hale)

Spend some time charting the life-shaping experiences that have influenced your servant heart. As you do so, pray that you can expunge the negatives and accentuate the positives.

True service can be painful, and we should be prepared for that. As Peter explained, "But if you suffer for doing good and you endure it, this is commendable before God. To this you were called, because Christ suffered for you, leaving you an example, that you should follow in his steps."[14]

[1] Jn. 12:25,26.

[2] 2 Cor. 9:12.

[3] Acts 13:2b.

[4] William Barclay, *New Testament Words* (London: SCM Press, 1964), 178.

[5] Eph. 2:10.

[6] Mt. 10:8b.

[7] Col. 3:23,24.

[8] Rom. 12:10b–11.

[9] Rick Warren, *The Purpose Driven Life* (Grand Rapids: Zondervan, 2002), 229. I thoroughly commend Purpose 4, entitled "You were shaped for serving God", in this excellent book.

[10] 1 Pet. 2:9.

[11] These are described in a most helpful way in Charles R. Swindoll, *Improving Your Serve* (London: Hodder and Stoughton, 1983), ch. 13, 194–210.

[12] J.E. O'Day, *Know Your Spiritual Gifts* (Downers Grove, IL: IVP, 2003).

[13] Rev. 3:15.

[14] 1 Pet. 2:20b–21.

7

Assess What Really Drives Your Choices

"Oh, that my ways were steadfast in obeying your decrees! Then I would not be put to shame when I consider all your commands."
(Ps. 119:5,6)

Outline

The material in this "time out" chapter leads you through a process of reflecting on the major choices you have made in your life to discover what motivated these choices.

The Christian worldview: What is distinctive about the Christian worldview, and how is it affected by external influences?

The psalmist's perspective: How does Psalm 19 challenge us to see that the God of the universe and of the Bible wants us to have his perspective in our decision making?

Case studies: Reappraisal at a crossroads: What effects can we see in the lives of people who made decisions on mission, marriage and career, based on questionable criteria?

Biblical advice for making choices: The Bible is not a decision manual, but how does it help us make good decisions?

Saul: A fallen star: What can we learn from Saul, who from privileged beginnings fell into disobedience and disregarded God's purpose for his life?

The Christian worldview

Christianity has been described as "a religion of motives". Yet few of us are keen to delve too deeply into our own motives. In part that is because we don't take much time for self-appraisal. Many of us are also uncomfortable with any form of introspection, worried perhaps about what we might find. But we need to remember that "All a man's ways seem innocent to him, but motives are weighed by the LORD"[1] or, in the words of Thomas à Kempis, "Man sees your actions, but God your motives." It often takes some form of crisis – physical, emotional or spiritual – to bring us to think more deeply about our motives and reflect on decisions past and present. There are good grounds, however, for not waiting until we reach a crossroads to seek to understand what has (to date) driven our big decisions in areas such as discipleship, work, partner, location, church, family and finances. This requires that we answer some searching questions. How well do you know yourself? How honest are you in assessing yourself? Are you willing to analyse the consequences of your decisions, good and bad? Your answers to these types of question will much depend on your worldview, so that's where we must start.

Although we may not be able to articulate it as such, each one of us has a worldview. Our worldview is the lens through which we view our lives, and it is the cumulative result of all of our experiences and how we have interpreted them. In short, it's our perspective on life – and that perspective determines how we react to everything that happens. Belief always determines behaviour. Most people, however, never think about their view of life in any systematic way. So while anyone can choose a worldview of their own, most adopt the default view that comes from friends, community, the media, pundits and other external sources. This default view in our culture has a massive impact on the choices that people make in all aspects of life. It can (and does) determine the nature of relationships, it promotes a popular secular morality, it influences financial choices, it shapes thinking on the family, it breeds cynicism about religious faith and so much more. Sadly, this worldview also infiltrates the thoughts and behaviour of many Christians – more than they would ever admit or even realize.

For our purposes here, we will look at two basic worldviews. The first view regards life as being merely the sum of a series of disconnected events and arbitrary experiences. Life, according to this view, has no overarching purpose. This perspective is common in the world around us. It may be disguised under new titles, but it's not new. Solomon summarized it in these grim words. "'Meaningless! Meaningless!' says the Teacher. 'Utterly meaningless! Everything is meaningless.'"[2] This view of life essentially leaves God out of the equation, such that humankind has no expectation that God is at work in any way. People make their own choices and are accountable only to themselves. The second worldview is entirely different. It's the Christian perspective that sees life as full of purpose. The basic premise is that God is in control of both the affairs of the world and the lives of his people. As Paul says, "And we know that in all things God works for the good of those who love him, who have been called according to his purpose."[3] If you hold this worldview, how should it affect your decisions? Firstly, you have to allow God to be centrally involved in them at all times – for many of us, unfortunately, this is clearly not the case. Secondly, the Christian needs to be aware that all choices have consequences, and he or she needs to be prepared to prayerfully consider these consequences, both before making a decision and afterwards. The following verses from Proverbs describe some of the serious consequences of rejecting God in our decision processes. "For they hated knowledge and chose not to fear the LORD. They rejected my advice and paid no attention when I corrected them. That is why they must eat the bitter fruit of living their own way. They must experience the full terror of the path they have chosen."[4] We will return to this question of looking to God for wisdom and advice. Thirdly, the Christian worldview requires us to live a life of faith and to trust the Lord to inform and guide all our decisions. This in itself is a powerful witness to the world around us. Think, for example, of how Paul viewed his imprisonment. "Now I want you to know, brothers, that what has happened to me has really served to advance the gospel."[5] Indeed it had – not least because the guards chained to him served in four hour shifts, captive to his witness!

REFLECTION:

C.S. Lewis brilliantly sums up what it looks like to have a Christian worldview. "I believe in Christianity as I believe that the sun has risen not only because I see it, but because by it I see everything else." How do you make decisions in the light of God's revelation? How would you explain your worldview to an unbeliever? Are there elements of the secular worldview that have crept into how you view your life and the world around you?

The psalmist's perspective

Psalm 19 clearly sets out the link between the God of the universe and the nature of our lives as his servants. While the case studies in the next section below illustrate the consequences faced by people whose decisions were based on a worldview affected by secularism, they cannot cover all of the possibilities. So it is important to understand the key scriptural principles. C.S. Lewis had high praise for Psalm 19: "I take it to be the greatest poem in the Psalter and one of the greatest lyrics in the world." As you read the psalm, look for its three related themes.

The skies: In verses 1–6, David looks upwards and marvels at the broad sweep of God's "wordless" revelation in the universe. He sees God's glory everywhere. "There is no speech or language where their voice is not heard."[6] Those with a Christian worldview see God's revelation, which is universal and rich in knowledge, daily. Others look upwards for astrological insights that are not part of this revelation – a fact we would do well to remember when looking for guidance for our lives. For there are things that the heavens do not declare. In David's day, the sun was the principal god of the Egyptians – but, as we see in this psalm, the sun is merely one of God's servants, following the path he has set for it to follow. Derek Kidner draws attention to another beautiful parallel. In the skies we see the path of the sun, while in the Scriptures we see the path of the Son – an even stronger source of light, love and life whose absence from our lives means darkness, desertion and death.[7]

The Scriptures: Verses 7–11 serve as a transition between the other two sections. Looking up is good, but it is not enough. Just as the heavens declare the glory of God, the Scriptures spell out the will of God. Those with a Christian perspective will see that while the sun dominates the sky by day, the Scriptures are designed to dominate and guide human life at all times. Both impart life. The sun's powerful heat strikes fear, as does the testing and purifying power of Scripture. Unlike the sun, however, Scripture exists not only to be admired, but also to be obeyed. Psalm 19 sets out seven ways that Scripture should impact the servant, including "reviving the soul", "making wise", "giving joy", "giving light" and so on. Are you allowing the Scriptures to work on your life in these ways? How would you fare if God showed you how he compared your life against clear scriptural standards?

The soul: The final verses (12–14) complete the extraordinary loop that links heavenly glory and earthly humility. These verses further explain the effect that the combined witness of the skies and the Scripture should have on Christians. It is clear from Psalm 19 that we should give God the same place in our hearts as he holds in the universe. And we should give Jesus the same place in our lives as he holds at the Father's side. David also struggles with the personal implications of these startling revelations. He prays, "Keep your servant also from wilful sins; may they not rule over me."[8] But David is also encouraged, as we should be, by the bounty of God's grace. He knows that God will help him, as he pleads, "May the words of my mouth and the meditation of my heart be pleasing in your sight, O LORD, my Rock and my Redeemer."[9] If the words of this verse became your goal and motivation in making decisions, what might change in your life?

CASE STUDIES:
Reappraisal at a crossroads

It is only in practice that we work out our principles – or ignore them. The following three case studies look at the lives of Christians who took different routes to finding out, too late, that they had in fact ignored their Christian principles in making major decisions. I have seen many similar cases in a variety of contexts. Can you identify with any of these situations? None of us finds it easy to admit that we were wrong – even to ourselves, but God "will bring to light what is hidden in darkness and will expose the motives of men's hearts".[10]

Roger and Sue were young teachers in tough urban schools. They had both been committed to Christian mission since their teenage years. Youth fellowships, holiday clubs and summer camps all had their active support. They enthusiastically attended every missionary convention in their area and had maintained an active correspondence with missionaries in Africa for several years. Shortly after their marriage they talked with their church leaders and asked for prayer about the possibility of doing missionary work in Africa. Their leaders were not surprised to hear of this interest, but they were concerned that the couple were a bit immature and too focused on the apparent glamour of overseas service. They all agreed to pray about the situation for six months. After much heart searching, Roger and Sue convinced their leaders and a mission society that they had a call to Africa and that their motives were the right ones. They had a difficult first year, learning a new language, dealing with the poor local infrastructure and the frustrations over getting things done, the painfully slow pace of life, homesickness and frequent bouts of poor health. Roger wrote home, "I thought we knew about all these things, but no briefing can fully prepare you for this – you have to experience it firsthand. Pray that we will be patient and mature in how we handle these lovely people." A year later things were no better, and they were privately admitting to themselves that this type of pioneering work was not what they thought it was. Progress in their work was slow,

they were unprepared and they felt that the reports they sent
to supporters back home were very low-key and mundane
compared with what had initially inspired them. They took some
time to reassess their motives and had to admit that the prospect
of Africa had seemed like a desirable escape from their difficult
school jobs at home. While they didn't feel that the aura of
missionary service was the primary influence in their call, they
did accept that it was a form of escapism. It took them quite a
few months to come to terms with their sense of failure and
potential loss of face. But they decided that they had to face up
to their mistake and learn from the experience. Their supporters
and close friends alike admired their courage in admitting all of
this. Roger and Sue returned home to a welcoming church where
they were involved in effective Christian service for many years
thereafter – the better for having honestly faced what had really
driven their decision to go to Africa.

Tony always had plenty of female friends. He was a
handsome, witty and intelligent young Christian man who
mixed well with everybody. He was also a great sportsman, and
proud of it. His leadership qualities were evident to all
throughout school and college. Those assessing his performance
described him as "A born leader; a distinctive natural talent; a
sure-fire success prospect in whatever he does in the future".
Tony's family background was a modest one, and he was the
first of his extended family to go to college. Life at home was a
struggle financially, mainly due to his father's persistent ill
health. Without scholarships his further education would have
been very difficult. If Tony had an Achilles heel, it was money
– he envied those who had it, and especially those who had it
in abundance. Tony married Judy shortly after leaving college.
She was almost the female equivalent of Tony in her many
attributes, except that she was much less enthusiastic about
sport. The couple gave little thought to God's guidance about
their marriage, not least because everybody thought that it was
a natural match. And Tony thought so too, of course – not least
because Judy's family had been very wealthy for three
generations. Among the wedding gifts lavished on the couple

were a splendid furnished home set in two acres within a rural setting, an appropriate sports car for each of them and a suitably large deposit in a bank account. As Judy's father put it, "We have to get them off to a good start – with God's blessing, of course. It's only money." All of this blew Tony's mind, and he decided to take a year off to enjoy it all. Judy was not keen on this, as she was on the fast track in a corporate finance career and a very driven individual. As the months went by Tony's tan developed nicely, his fitness improved, his tennis was great, and his golf handicap went down in direct proportion to the increase in tension at home. "Tony, I had no idea that you would react to my parents' generosity in this way. I can't believe this is happening. Is this why you married me? We should pray about this." In fact, Tony had no interest in praying about it – life was too good for that. Nor did he want to admit what his true motivation had been. Judy's parents were devastated when, after six months, she confided that the marriage was not going at all well. Things came to a head three months later. Judy suggested a trial separation unless Tony could come to his senses and start earning a living within a month. An unconfirmed rumour that one of his friendships at the tennis club was less than platonic prompted her ultimatum. For the first time ever, Tony was truly shaken. He had to admit that while he did love Judy, he had loved the prospect of her family money even more. He denied any affairs, and in this he was truthful. There was enough Christian sentiment left in him to enable him to see that he had misled Judy, and he agreed to the separation. Sadly, a high-profile, messy and acrimonious divorce followed which damaged them both as well as the cause of Christ in the local community. In their case there was no way back from the original bad decision, and both struggled with their Christian faith for many years afterwards.

Hunter was a brilliant academic. He combined his teaching, research and administrative skills in an unusual way. His work on genetics was widely respected, and he constantly struggled with the many demands on his time from his own university and from research communities around the world. He was a gifted

communicator, and many conference planners vied to get him on their programmes. In his early thirties, when his career began to take off, he regularly prayed that he would be able to manage the various pushes and pulls on his time. He had seen several other Christian friends in similar circumstances drift out of God's service. He told his wife June, "I need to plan my Christian activities as carefully as the rest of my work – I have to be disciplined with my time. It's the only way." He asked June to remind him of this pledge as often as was necessary. He checked his motives regularly at this formative stage and established some good patterns. He led a Bible study with his peers, was influential in a seekers group in his church and was a fearless witness. However, life thereafter gathered pace. He faced the classic academic dilemma as to what his job really was. His professorship entailed a core of responsibilities, but he had a great deal of discretion as to how he developed his job outside the university. As he progressively developed this aspect of his job, he could always justify his activities as being in his colleagues' interests as well as his own. Chairing professional committees, liaising with international research sponsors and his many other roles required much weekend travel. By age forty-five, his motives had migrated to building a career, albeit as a Christian – but his wider commitment to Christian service had all but disappeared. He was a rare visitor at church. June's reminders of his pledge were futile, and she was also influenced by the lifestyle benefits that came from international travel and greater financial security. As a resource for God, Hunter was almost lost. He did witness, but not consistently, and he found it was easier to be silent in many situations. But life was good, and in his early fifties he was a stellar success – by the measures of honorary degrees and visiting fellowships in world-renowned institutions. Life changed dramatically for him at age fifty-five, when he had a serious heart attack. During an extensive recuperation period, he undertook a fundamental reappraisal of his life. In his vulnerability he experienced a crisis of conscience regarding his stewardship of the resources with which God had blessed him. He knew that he had consciously allowed his

motives to be corrupted. He had taken "building a career" too far, and pursuing this goal had driven him way off course. Everything he had worked for was really for himself, regardless of how he had dressed it up in the past. He wanted to get back on track with God's plan. This resolve stuck. He returned to a restructured and less demanding career and thereafter devoted much of his life to the work of medical missions. His efforts were fruitful and blessed by God as he used his talents for God's glory.

Biblical advice for making choices

God wants us to look to him when we make decisions, and therefore the Bible is full of advice to help us make wise choices. While the Bible does specifically mention many of life's major decisions, it gives us broad principles rather than detailed instructions for every eventuality. This foundational wisdom should guide all of our choices. The book of Proverbs is particularly helpful in this regard. Table 7.1 highlights some of the Bible's wisdom for those facing crossroads decisions.

Table 7.1 Wise words for making choices

Ask God for wisdom:
" . . . and if you call out for insight and cry aloud for understanding . . . then you will understand the fear of the LORD and find the knowledge of God."[11]

Work on your relationship with Christ:
"I am the vine; you are the branches. If a man remains in me and I in him, he will bear much fruit; apart from me you can do nothing."[12]

Get your priorities right:
"Commit to the LORD whatever you do, and your plans will succeed."[13]

Listen to good advice:
"The way of a fool seems right to him, but a wise man listens to advice."[14]

Money is not everything:
"Whoever trusts in his riches will fall, but the righteous will thrive like a green leaf."[15] "The blessing of the LORD brings wealth, and he adds no trouble to it."[16]

Take some risks:
"Now faith is being sure of what we hope for and certain of what we do not see. This is what the ancients were commended for."[17]

Commit your choices to God:
"Commit your way to the LORD; trust in him and he will do this: He will make your righteousness shine like the dawn, the justice of your cause like the noonday sun."[18]

But what does God call us to do when we realize we have made a wrong choice? As we have seen, some of the choices that we make are irreversible, as are some choices that others have made for us in our earlier lives. Again, there are biblical characters from whom we can learn. Lot, for example, ultimately had to listen to the word of God and flee from the city of Sodom. In some situations, the best thing to do when we have taken a wrong turn is to get out if at all possible. When Peter realized what he had done in denying the Lord, he saw that he needed to repent and devote the rest of his life to the Lord's service. Paul persecuted Christ and then accepted God's grace. "The grace of our Lord was poured out on me abundantly, along with the faith and love that are in Christ Jesus."[19] When God forgave and accepted Paul, a transformed life of service began – from which we all benefit to this day. What an encouragement, from such improbable beginnings, this is for us all.

REFLECTION:

Identify a decision that you are currently considering and try applying the Bible's wisdom (see Table 7.1, above) to this situation. Reflect on your motives and whether or not you need to also rectify a wrong choice.

Saul: A fallen star

We end this chapter on a solemn note as we consider the life of a complex, talented and able man whose motives became very confused and whose fall from grace was quite spectacular. The life of Saul, Israel's first king, was full of crossroads – not all of which were, apparently, obvious to him at the time. A series of self-centred decisions resulted in his rapid and irreversible decline as God's initial vision for him faded away. He is one of the most striking and tragic figures in the Old Testament. He ended life with material wealth but moral poverty. We can summarize his life story (told in 1 Samuel 9 – 31) in three phases.

Promising: Saul got a great start in life. He was handsome and displayed many commendable qualities including modesty and generosity. We also see in his love for David and Jonathan that he had the capacity to love others deeply. When God called him to be king, he also equipped him for the job. The prophet Samuel assured him, "do whatever your hand finds to do, for God is with you".[20] Saul commanded the respect of a large following, "accompanied by valiant men whose hearts God had touched".[21] Everything in his kingdom was not rosy, of course, and some doubted him. But his natural gifts and supernatural call and equipping placed him in a good position to lead his people with distinction and operate within Lord's plan to bless them.

Declining: In spite of Saul's great start, the rot set in quite early in his reign. God's intention was that Saul would free Israel from the Philistines, but it was no time before Saul started to take things into his own hands and went about trying to free Israel in ways that were contrary to God's plan. Saul was wilful, disobedient and deceitful in equal measure. God's displeasure is only too evident in his message to Samuel. "I am grieved that I have made Saul king, because he has turned away from me and has not carried out my instructions."[22] Shortly afterwards, when Samuel anoints David, we read, "Now the Spirit of the LORD had departed from Saul, and an evil spirit from the LORD tormented him."[23] His decline leads to his making three attempts to kill David – a mutinous act against God's

anointed king. What brought on Saul's decline? Sidlaw Baxter summarizes the progressive stages in his ruin: "First self-sensitiveness, then self-assertiveness, then self-centredness, increasingly issuing in self-destructiveness".[24] During his decline Saul was not without his moments of telling self-assessment. For example, after David had spared his life, he declared, "Surely I have acted like a fool and have erred greatly."[25] This could, in effect, have been his epitaph – since such moments of insight did not lead to any material change in his behaviour. Foolish he was, and foolish he remained.

Failing: We can see the full extent of Saul's failure in his final acts – looking for wisdom from a witch and ultimately committing suicide. It's doubtful whether Saul ever really surrendered to God, in that he failed to behave as one anointed to do God's will. How easy it is for us, also, to deceive ourselves and "do our own thing" under the umbrella of Christian discipleship and service. Saul lacked neither opportunity nor talent – but they were not enough. Saul was disobedient on many counts and completely centred on himself. He had much knowledge, but little wisdom. As Sandra Carey reminds us, "Never mistake knowledge for wisdom. One helps you make a living; the other helps you make a life." Saul's was a fruitless life, and he took wrong turns at several of his most important crossroads. Sadly, he never found a way back to God.

SELAH:

Take some time to reflect on the big decisions you have made in the past. Were any of them made with hidden motives – motives that you have never confronted but now feel compelled to address?

What can you learn from Saul's life?

As you reflect and repent, remember that "The Lord is not slow in keeping his promise, as some understand slowness. He is patient with you, not wanting anyone to perish, but everyone to come to repentance."[26]

[1] Prov. 16:2.

[2] Ecc. 1:2.

[3] Rom. 8:28.

[4] Prov. 1:29–31 (NLT).

[5] Phil. 1:12.

[6] Ps. 19:3.

[7] Derek Kidner, *Psalms 1–73* (London: Inter-Varsity Press, 1973), 98,99.

[8] Ps. 19:13a.

[9] Ps. 19:14.

[10] 1 Cor. 4:5b.

[11] Prov. 2:3,5.

[12] Jn. 15:5.

[13] Prov. 16:3.

[14] Prov. 12:15.

[15] Prov. 11:28.

[16] Prov. 10.22.

[17] Heb. 11:1,2.

[18] Ps. 37:5,6.

[19] 1 Tim. 1:14.

[20] 1 Sam. 10:7.

[21] 1 Sam. 10:26.

[22] 1 Sam. 15:11.

[23] 1 Sam. 16:14.

[24] J. Sidlaw Baxter, *Mark these Men* (London: Marshall, Morgan & Scott, 1949), 30,31.

[25] 1 Sam. 26:21.

[26] 2 Pet. 3:9.

8

Listen to Good Advice

"The fear of the LORD is the beginning of wisdom;
all who follow his precepts have good
understanding. To him belongs eternal praise."
(Ps. 111:10)

Outline

At some time or another we all need advice. But do you know where to go to seek good advice? And, when you do receive good advice, do you listen and respond?

Gauge your response: What is your pattern for responding to advice?

Remember the source: What do we need to know about true wisdom from God?

Crossroads advice: How can we distinguish between advice at a crossroads and advice that takes us to a crossroads?

Stop, look, listen: What are the "rules of the crossroad"?

Christian character: Three pieces of advice: What can we learn about growing, behaving and trusting that will help us to develop Christian character in the context of crossroads experiences?

A dialogue with God: Apply what you have learned so far: how might you have handled this particular crossroads situation?

Gauge your response

Do you value good advice? How has the advice of others influenced the big decisions in your life to date? All of us respond to advice in different ways – depending on the particular circumstances in which we receive it, our personalities, the credentials of the person giving the advice, the specific advice proffered and the manner in which it is given. While the poet Samuel Taylor Coleridge wrote that "Advice is like snow: the softer it falls, the longer it dwells upon and the deeper it sinks into the mind", Paul Tournier, by contrast, said that "Every piece of advice conceals a veiled criticism, unless it has been asked for." How often do we feel that sense of bristling and defensiveness when we receive advice? And how often, even when we seek advice, do we question its tone and content?

When it comes to taking advice about spiritual matters, most of us feel the same reticence. We are not always open to advice from God or to good advice from his people based on his word. Over many years of conversations and pastoral engagement with fellow Christians, I have observed that people's responses to advice fall into the broad categories set out in Table 8.1. If you see yourself there somewhere, quietly acknowledge that before the Lord and think about the consequences for heeding good advice in the future.

Table 8.1 Types of Christian response to advice

Collectors consult almost everybody they know, irrespective of their qualifications to advise, and in general make a show of telling everybody else (in confidence) what advice they have received. They often follow the advice that gets the majority vote.

Selectors know a group of people who will give them the advice they want to hear. They steer clear of anyone who might advise to the contrary. They are not really seeking good or balanced advice, only acceptable advice – especially if it flatters their ego.

Loners rarely ask for advice from anyone. They commonly feel that their decisions are so personal and complex that few others are qualified to help. Sometimes they do not trust others with their burden or do not value another opinion – including God's.

Checkers make up their own minds before they seek advice but feel a need to ratify it with a few friendly advisers – basically as a process of self-reinforcing. They get hurt if nobody agrees with them.

Receivers sift the advice given with care and prayer. They place a premium on good advice from experienced and wise people. They often form life-long bonds with their group of counsellors. Above all they study the Bible and have meaningful conversations with God about their decisions.

Think about how you have received and processed advice in the past. Although many of us might be tempted to classify ourselves exclusively as "receivers", that is likely to be a delusion. Once you have identified your pattern, you are ready to address the next question. What are you open to being advised about? This is where our own view of our personal expertise comes in. For example, a Grand Prix racing driver sees little merit in taking beginner driving lessons; a brain surgeon is unlikely to gain much additional experience with a scalpel from being taught by a carpenter about his special skills with a chisel; nor is a theology professor likely to apply to retake Theology 101. While few of us would cite "Living the Christian Life" as our specialist subject in a quiz, many of us think that we have the general idea of how it is done and are not as open to good advice as we should be. I occasionally sing parts of different tunes as I work in my home office. My wife can usually vaguely recognize them – but if she were to ask me for the right key, the whole tune and the words, I would often be at a loss. So it is with us at times – we need more than the general idea to be able to live for Christ. For our whole lives to glorify God in tuneful praise, we need to know the whole song – we need good advice from the right sources.

Remember the source

Psalm 111:10 reminds us that God is the ultimate source of all Christian advice – and the first area in which we need wisdom and sound advice is in our relationship with God. A proper relationship with God is central to instructions such as the following: "Be very careful, then, how you live – not as unwise but as wise, making the most of every opportunity, because the days are evil."[1] When our focus is on God, we will exercise that care in our living and we will want true wisdom, recognizing that it only comes from one source. What else do we need to know about true wisdom?

It begins with the fear of the Lord: "The fear of the LORD is the beginning of knowledge, but fools despise wisdom and discipline."[2] Without such reverence we will not be receptive to God's word – a fact that helps to explain why so many Christians spend so little time reading the Bible. Is this true of you? But there are many rewards for this godly fear, including an increase in the quality of life, "Humility and the fear of the LORD bring wealth and honour and life"[3] and protection from evil, "The fear of the LORD leads to life: Then one rests content, untouched by trouble."[4]

It avoids the behaviour that God detests: The Bible is very clear about what is unacceptable to God. These behaviours include listing lying, pride and deceit[5] and the worship of the wicked, "The LORD detests the sacrifice of the wicked, but the prayer of the upright pleases him."[6] But God measures what we do not do as well, and many of us need to take solemn heed if we are ignoring his word: "If anyone turns a deaf ear to the law, even his prayers are detestable."[7] Hypocritical lives that flaunt biblical teaching are futile – and are already exposed to God's eye. It is pure folly to try to avoid God's advice or to try to justify behaviour that he will always detest.

REFLECTION:

St Augustine once said, "The Holy Scriptures are our letters from home." Are you eager to read the Bible, searching its pages for news from the One you love? Prayerfully examine your own heart. Is your attitude towards God's advice pleasing to him?

Crossroads advice

There are two circumstances in particular that drive us to seek good advice. The first is when we realize we are at a crossroads, with life-shaping decisions to make – both large and small – and we are searching for some light to be shed on the way ahead. The second is when we are given advice of such significance, and which has such an impact on our lives, that it actually brings us to a crossroads because it forces us to make a decision. The following biblical examples illustrate these two situations with advice that applies to our lifestyle and to our service.

Crossroads now: To one degree or another, all of us face crossroads daily as we are challenged to live for Christ in a hostile world. The many choices we make affect our witness, our relationships with God and other people, our personal growth, our joy, peace and contentment and so on. These decisions determine our effectiveness as Christians in the context in which God has placed us. In 1 Peter, the apostle gives essential instructions to a community of persecuted believers. His teaching is relevant for every Christian who lives in an ungodly culture – and, sadly, that is true of the vast majority of us. "Live such good lives among the pagans that, though they accuse you of doing wrong, they may see your good deeds and glorify God on the day he visits us."[8] How can we do this? Peter offers much sound advice here. We need to begin by confirming our sense of identity as "a chosen people, a royal priesthood, a holy nation, a people belonging to God."[9] We must also make sure that our relationships with family, believers and with the authorities are in order. Finally, we must be prepared to suffer. This latter advice in particular often falls on deaf ears in our generation. Many Christians actively pursue "suffering avoidance strategies" in their work and wider community by being silent when they should be speaking, compliant when they should be resisting, cautious when they should be courageous. I know people of whom this has been true for years, people who evidently find Peter's words on this aspect of discipleship unacceptable. "But even if you should suffer for what is right, you are blessed."[10] What do we do with such advice from God? We should all ask ourselves this question, for someday he will ask us himself. In the words of Henry Ward Beecher, "If a man cannot be a Christian where he is, he cannot be a Christian anywhere."

Crossroads ahead: The instructions that Paul gave to Timothy about Christian service are typical of biblical teaching that leads us to crossroads. The decision at such a crossroads is this: how much of ourselves are we willing to give to God? Timothy had made a good start, having been involved in several important missions with Paul and having gained his respect. But his responsibilities were about to increase – hence the extensive instructions from Paul that were to influence his life thereafter. Paul's pointed yet gracious advice brings Timothy to a crossroads at which he needs to determine the focus, shape and purpose of his life. Paul tells Timothy to obey the commandments and live a life "that conforms to the glorious gospel of the blessed God".[11] The example he set would be the basis of his testimony – and it had to be a good one in order for him to be effective. Paul advises Timothy to honour God, to avoid shipwreck by holding on to the faith, to have a good conscience and to be prayerful in all things. Paul knew all too well that lack of prayer leads to distance from the Lord. Some in Timothy's community were defecting from the Christian faith, and so Paul also urges him to persevere – converting early enthusiasm to staying power. Paul knows that Timothy will need to stay focused, to remember who he serves and who he is trying to please: "No-one serving as a soldier gets involved in civilian affairs – he wants to please his commanding officer."[12] Only as he perseveres with God will Timothy be able to discern the counterfeits that display a form of godliness but are powerless about which Paul further warns. Underlying all of the wisdom Paul imparts is a strong note of encouragement. "But as for you, continue in what you have learned and have become convinced of, because you know those from whom you learned it."[13] All of this advice gives Timothy both direction and reassurance for his role as a Christian leader. God urges us, too, to press on from our crossroads along the route of obedience.

Stop, look, listen

At many crossroads you will find traffic lights – usually red, amber (or yellow) and green. Think about the spiritual decisions that currently face you. As you prayerfully approach these crossroads, try applying this metaphor to help clarify your choices.

Red: Stop, do not go ahead. You should see a red light in a situation where a certain course of action is clearly contrary to God's teaching. Such a warning is a gift from the Lord to protect you against a wrong course of action, and you would be well advised neither to challenge nor ignore that advice. When you heed the red light and stop, you will probably also be able to see some of the reasons for it. Consider the consequences had you gone ahead and thank God for this signal.

Amber: Caution, slow down. When you are not sure whether or not to proceed, it is always safest to await another signal. When the advice you have is inconclusive, take time for further prayer and reflection. Perhaps you have been speeding single-mindedly towards this crossroads. Are you perhaps not fully prepared to take this step? Do you need to pay more attention to another area of your spiritual growth first? Is it a matter of waiting for God's timing? Be prepared for the fact that the next signal could be either red or green.

Green: Go now. The way ahead is clear (even if you cannot yet see all of the bends in the road ahead). You will feel freedom to take this route, confident in the knowledge that your choice has a sound biblical mandate and that your motives are sound. We often need a measure of boldness to actually go forward at a green light – make sure that you are not still waiting before a green light when the Lord has already told you to go.

REFLECTION:

> Spiritual growth consists most in the growth of the root, which
> is out of sight. (Matthew Henry)

As we seek to follow God, we need to keep in mind the clear distinction between activity and spiritual progress. Where is most of your growth? Is it above ground for others to see and admire? Or are you deeply rooted in the Lord?

Christian character: Three pieces of advice

Thomas à Kempis once said, "Be not angry that you can not make others as you wish them to be, since you can not make yourself as you wish to be." This humbling truth reminds us that we should focus our attention on listening, not judging, and that we should be more prescriptive about ourselves than we are about others. We approach the following three pieces of advice – about growing, behaving and trusting – with that spirit of humility. These critical elements of Christian character relate here to crossroads experiences. It is more difficult to take this kind of advice if we are in poor spiritual health, if we have recently behaved in a way that has not honoured God, or if we are not continuing to remind ourselves of the sovereignty and permanence of God.

Growing – attend to your spiritual health: Just as a poor relationship with the Lord can lead to poor decisions, so the converse is equally true. For example, Daniel was able to stand strong for God in the crisis of his captivity because of his close relationship with him. Paul, too, was able to endure endless trials and persecutions because he had made a specific commitment to the Lord and was empowered by the Spirit. The Bible gives us lots of advice about how to develop and maintain our spiritual health. If we stay with the medical analogy, we need to start with our immune system – our spiritual capacity to resist threats such as temptation, persecution or contemporary philosophies that detract from God. We need to be proactive about this, as James reminds us. "Submit yourselves, then, to God. Resist the devil, and he will flee from you."[14] Paul also reminds us that we need to be on the defensive. "Put on the full armour of God so that you can take your stand against the devil's schemes."[15] Regular physical exercise is one of the keys to building a healthy immune system. Spiritual exercise and discipline, in the areas of prayer, Bible study and service, are no less important. "We do not want you to become lazy, but to imitate those who through faith and patience inherit what has been promised."[16] Part of obeying this mandate involves actively deploying our spiritual gifts and fulfilling our role in the body of Christ. We need to understand that this exercise is time-bound by our own life and health span, and the Lord reminds us: "As long as it is day, we must do the work of him who sent me. Night is coming when no-one can work."[17] Good health requires not just work, but rest as well. Many active Christians leave too little time for rejuvenation and recovery. Jesus set us a good example by the periods of retreat he took. Luke, a first-hand witness, tells us, "But Jesus often withdrew to lonely places and prayed."[18] Clearly there is value in both solitude and in good company, and doing something different often helps to restore our energy as well. The final ingredient of spiritual health is a healthy diet. We hear lots of medical and commercial advice on diet and many people, Christians among them, are passionately interested in alternative diets to improve their physical health. The biblical advice is more direct and allows for less experimentation with what is good for us. In order to reap the benefits of this wise advice, however, we need to follow it passionately. "Like newborn babies, crave pure spiritual milk, so that by it you may grow up in your salvation, now that you have tasted that the Lord is good."[19] As Jesus himself said, "It is written: 'Man does not live on bread alone, but on every word that comes from the mouth of God.'"[20] One of our greatest challenges is to eat a balanced diet of the right food for our souls. The age of mass media and global communications provides us with vast volumes of food that seem attractive but are never able to sustain us. What a blessing spiritual health

brings to us and to others around us. We should never think that the Lord is indifferent to our spiritual health.

Behaving – watch your tongue: We speak in many different contexts, but it is important to remember that God is always our most attentive listener. The tongue is a mighty force – for good or evil. It can bring comfort or cause distress; it can build up with encouragement or destroy with damning criticism; it can shed light or promote darkness. The tongue is capable of causing many crossroads. For example, Peter's oaths and curses at the time of his denial were the expression of a crisis in his life; the hollow and deceptive philosophies that were taught to the Colossians diverted many from their Christian faith; and John the Baptist, in declaring that Jesus must become greater and he must become less, was anticipating a major change in his future ministry. In each of these situations tongues were used in very different, but equally influential, ways. Such, then, is the power of the tongue that we need to look carefully at the biblical advice on this aspect of Christian behaviour. The book of James is a good source, since he is particularly concerned about the sins of speech. These words of warning are direct and to the point: "Everyone should be quick to listen, slow to speak and slow to become angry, for man's anger does not bring about the righteous life that God desires."[21] Or, as C.H. Spurgeon graphically described it, "Some men's tongues bite more than their teeth." The core issue here is self-control, and James recognizes that "We all stumble in many ways. If anyone is never at fault in what he says, he is a perfect man, able to keep his whole body in check."[22] Because this small part of our bodies can have a disproportionate impact for good or ill, its power needs to be controlled. James likens the tongue to a bridle controlling a horse and a rudder steering the course of a ship. In recognizing its power we also acknowledge the tongue's destructive potential – and not just in a dispassionate way, as if we were never the guilty party. James uses the illustration of fire and its effects. "The tongue also is a fire, a world of evil among the parts of the body. It corrupts the whole person, sets the whole course of his life on fire, and is itself set on fire by

hell."[23] Like the forest fire, it can rapidly get out of control and its effects can be widespread. Every part of our character can be stained by the tongue, and the lives of those who speak and who hear can be destroyed. While no one can tame the tongue, God can – and we must be willing to let him tame it. Effective Christian discipleship requires that our tongues are tamed. Proverbs tells us, "The tongue that brings healing is a tree of life, but a deceitful tongue crushes the spirit."[24] Taming our tongues begins in the heart. As Jesus reminds us in this sobering prediction, it is the content of our hearts that comes out of our mouths. "But I tell you that men will have to give account on the day of judgment for every careless word they have spoken."[25] There are three things that don't come back – the spent arrow, the spoken word and the lost opportunity.

Trusting – be assured by his permanence: Of the many needs that a Christian may have when facing a crossroads, I can think of none more important than to know the truth that "Jesus Christ is the same yesterday and today and for ever."[26] In an age of dramatic change, who else remains the same? This profound yet simple verse is full of challenge, comfort and assurance. One of the great themes in the letter to the Hebrews is the assurance of our access to God – who is unchangeable in character and nature. Our society places a limited value on "sameness" – most people are searching for something new and novel. In sharp contrast, Jesus Christ remains the same. We have our ups and downs; we claim to be morning people or night owls; we are unreliable and inconsistent. Even if we have a reputation for being steady, the "same" in all circumstances, we still change through age, health and so on. God, however, never changes: "But you remain the same, and your years will never end."[27] This is a prayer for those who were close to the end of their endurance, as God gave his eternal commitment to his servants regardless of circumstances. For us, Jesus Christ is the same as when we accepted him, as when we ignored and rejected him, as when he was bypassed and his will flaunted. Of broken human relationships we often say, "Things will never be the same again" – but not so with the Lord! What grace and love

are contained in a promise like this: "I the LORD do not change. So you, O descendants of Jacob, are not destroyed."[28] With Spurgeon, we should say that "Nothing bids me to my Lord like a strong belief in His changeless love." Jesus Christ is the same because he cannot change. His love, holiness and judgement are as they have always been – not subject to compromise, negotiation or arbitration. He is the same God who forgave David and Jacob, raised Lazarus, blessed Moses as a leader, broke through Paul's resistance and stilled the storm. How has God helped you in the past? Too many of us have short-term memories, but God encourages us for the future when we remember his acts in the past. Samuel set up a physical reminder of God's care and provision. "Then Samuel took a stone and set it up . . . saying, 'Thus far has the LORD helped us.'"[29] We need to remember, too, that God can forgive our wrong actions in the past, revitalize our present and secure our future. Jesus Christ is the same forever, the Lord of eternity. This is the God who enables us to face our present and future crossroads, both great and small, with confidence. As Robert Murray McCheyne reminds us: "Live near to God, and all things will appear little to you in comparison with eternal realities."

A dialogue with God

Most of us engage in some form of conversation with the Lord over decisions we need to make. These dialogues may be long or short, comprehensive or partial. Most of us will enter into these consultations with an attitude that reflects our pattern for seeking advice (see Table 8.1, above). What patterns and attitudes do you see in the following "crossroads conversation"?

Context

Joe and Bernard had been friends since their college days. Joe joined the police and progressed through the ranks. He was very involved in youth work in his community, motivated by his desire to improve the opportunities for young people and by

his Christian faith. He was married to Mary, and they had three children. Bernard had started a security company with another friend shortly after leaving college, but now he owned his own company with about a hundred employees installing and maintaining alarm systems. His business was very successful, but the cost had been high. His work pressures had led to the failure of his marriage to Georgina. Joe had become very conscious of the contrast between their financial circumstances and was envious of Bernard's success. Moreover, Joe was not keen on the night work that was part of his police job, and Mary was increasingly worried about the risks involved. Bernard was a very aggressive businessman and not wholly honest in his dealings. Joe had heard one or two whispers about him in the course of his police work, but it was all hearsay. Bernard had often asked Joe to leave his career in the police and join him as a director in his business. On this occasion, Joe said that he would pray about his offer over the next week. "Fine," Bernard said, "if you feel you have to. But don't take more than a week – business is booming and this chance won't come again." Joe went off to look for advice.

Conversation

Joe: "It's a great offer, and we need the money," he told Mary. "Bernard doesn't share my faith, but neither do many of my colleagues in the police – and I don't completely trust them either. Maybe I'll talk to Bill first and see what he thinks – we're usually on the same wavelength." Mary and Joe agreed that they should pray together and ask God about this major decision. But they never quite got around to it – they were a bit too excited for that.
Bill: "Joe, all I can say is that I wish Bernard had made the same offer to me. Go for it – all of the other issues you mentioned are secondary. You're a man of experience, and you'll be able to handle Bernard. You meet his type every day."
Joe: "Thanks, Bill. You're probably right – but I have nagging doubts."

By day three Bill had still not prayed about the choice facing him. He told Mary, "I just want to get my own ideas clear first."
God: In the early hours of day four, Joe tossed and turned. "Joe, I haven't heard from you much on this matter. I have three questions for you. Do you feel comfortable working with Bernard, given your suspicions about his values? Are your reasons for leaving the police force good ones, given the witness you have been there and the good work you have done for me in the community? Are your money problems so significant that they should drive this choice?"
Joe: "Lord, I'm sorry for my silence. I can't sleep because of worrying about this. I need your advice more than anything else right now. Your questions are good ones and I haven't taken the time to set out the options before you – can you give me the right answers?"
God: "I already know all about your dilemma. Joe, the choice is yours – if only you would learn to trust me. I have been trying to speak to you in different ways, but you've resisted. This is the first real test of your strength. Why don't you answer my questions?"
Joe: By now it was day six, and Joe had found the answers. "Lord, you're right. My answers are: I'm not entirely comfortable with Bernard; I did know that you wanted me to be in the police; and no, I should not decide this on money alone. You've given me guidance, but I've been editing it over the past few days to suit myself. And I confess that I'm still wavering."

Conclusion

On the morning of day seven, Joe was driving to see Bernard to give him his response. But he was still unsure of his final decision. A call on his mobile interrupted his thoughts. His first inclination was to ignore it. When he did respond, however, he heard the voice of a senior colleague in a neighbouring police division. "Joe, we raided the premises of your friend Bernard last night. We've had him under surveillance for months through an insider working in his business. We plan to bring a dozen charges against him for fraud and corruption. The evidence against him looks very strong – my guess is that he'll get two to three years in prison. Just thought that you'd want to know." Stunned, Joe mumbled his thanks. He pulled his car into the next lay-by, wept and prayed for an hour and more. "What a deliverance! Thank you, Lord. I've known for days what your view of this was, but I was too stubborn and proud and self-centred to admit it. Please help me to learn from this."

SELAH:

> The doorstep to the temple of wisdom is a knowledge of our own ignorance. (C.H. Spurgeon)

Have you ever edited God's advice to make it more acceptable to you? What were, or are, the consequences of doing this?

> Character is what you are in the dark. (D.L. Moody)

What have you learned about growing, behaving and trusting that you can apply to current spiritual decisions with which you are wrestling?

---

1   Eph. 5:15,16.
2   Prov. 1:7.
3   Prov. 22:4.
4   Prov. 19:23.
5   Prov. 6:16–19.
6   Prov. 15:8.
7   Prov. 28:9.
8   1 Pet. 2:12.
9   1 Pet. 2:9.
10   1 Pet. 3:14.
11   1 Tim. 1:11.
12   2 Tim. 2:4.
13   2 Tim. 3:14.
14   Jas. 4:7.
15   Eph. 6:11.
16   Heb. 6:12.
17   Jn. 9:4.

[18] Lk. 5:16.
[19] 1 Pet. 2:2,3.
[20] Mt. 4:4.
[21] Jas. 1:19,20.
[22] Jas. 3:2.
[23] Jas. 3:6.
[24] Prov. 15:4.
[25] Mt. 12:36.
[26] Heb. 13:8.
[27] Ps. 102:27.
[28] Mal. 3:6.
[29] 1 Sam. 7:12.

9

Confirm that You Are Where God Wants You to Be

"I have set the LORD always before me. Because he is at my right hand, I shall not be shaken."
(Ps. 16:8)

Outline

True discipleship presumes that we would like to know that we are indeed where God wants us to be. But are we prepared to make the necessary adjustments?

Ask a disruptive question: Asking God where he wants us to be can be disruptive. Why is it important to ask this question?

Search for God's will: What does the Bible tell us about how we can know that we are walking in God's will?

People in the right place: Incidents from the lives of five biblical characters help to show us how God affirmed their roles and locations.

Journey to Nineveh: What is your "Nineveh"? And how can we recover from our disobedience?

Ask a disruptive question

"Lord, am I where you want me to be?" How often have you asked this potentially unsettling question? If your answer is "never" or "rarely", then you might find this chapter challenging. It's a valid question for every Christian disciple to ask in many different dimensions of our lives – for example, in terms of where you live, where you work and where you worship. Are you where God wants you to be in terms of your relationships with your family, your fellow Christians, your wider circle of friends? What about your state of mind, your attitudes and the balance of priorities in your life?

We ask the question because we want to follow God and honour him in all parts of our lives. But we have to be prepared for disruption, because God may well answer that we are not where he wants us to be in some or all of the areas cited above. This willingness to listen and to obey is the basis of our discipleship in this master/servant relationship. Our focus should always be on pleasing our master. Vance Havner captures the essence of this demanding and rewarding relationship: "Our Lord made discipleship hard and lost many prospective followers because he called them to a pilgrimage, not a parade – to a fight, not to a frolic." Posing and answering this vital question can in itself be a crossroads experience.

I have met many Christians who resist asking this question because they are terrified of the answer. So they live in fear, and probably disobedience, never being certain of God's appraisal of their lives. Why is it that we routinely accept the assessment of our earthly masters, but are so reluctant to hear from our heavenly one? Fear may not be the only explanation for that type of restricted relationship with the Lord. Some people, for example, try to keep their Christian faith and daily practice in separate compartments and do not want to contemplate any type of change that does not suit their chosen lifestyle. This can be due to inertia, or disobedience, or both. Some may firmly believe that they are where the Lord wants them to be theologically but show little interest in being where he wants

them to be in terms of their attitudes. Others have either perfected their resistance to God's prompting or suffer from being in a secure spiritual cocoon that shuts them off from any heavenly critique of their lives. There are some profound consequences for those who have no interest in knowing if they are where God wants them to be, as we will see in the lives of the following four people. The first three people are all at crossroads, while those in the fourth case have just passed one.

Jim is intelligent but lazy and fails to apply himself to most things in life. His career, church life and general relationships have suffered through a lifelong pattern of peaks and troughs. He never quite seems to settle anywhere. As a result he has never reached his potential and has grown cynical – especially about those who are less able but more successful than he is. He is forty years old, very discontented, and has no idea how he fits into God's plans. Opportunity, at least by his own standards, seems to have passed him by. It has never occurred to him to ask God whether he is where he wants him to be. He is content to be discontent. He is not great company, and he is an even less effective witness. He is a five-talent resource heading for a one-talent return.

David has been unhappy in his church for many years, but he is noted for his inertia – he simply doesn't like change. In the meantime, while he knows that it's wrong, he has developed advanced skills in criticism. Everybody who stands in the pulpit and most of the church leaders are subject to his "higher criticism". He is unhappy and unfulfilled. During holidays and at conventions he mixes with other Christian groups and benefits greatly. While he knows that he should change where he worships for his own spiritual health, he has learned to cope with, and shut off from, much of what is said and done in his church. He is in his own time warp. He has prayed selectively about his attitudes – mainly asking God to change everybody else. He has listened to God even more selectively. He knows that he is not where the Lord wants him – but he remains a thorn in the flesh to many of his fellow worshippers!

Veronica has faced relationship problems in her family since her father died seven years ago. Her two brothers and two

sisters-in-law all professed Christian faith, but none of them were champions of Christian grace – as became evident when they discovered the content of her late father's will. Since all of his family members were financially secure, he had directed almost all of his considerable wealth to Christian missions. While he had been very precise in most things, he was much less so concerning the valuable contents of his home. As a result, there was considerable family strife over the allocation of his possessions. As a single lady who had until recently lived in the family home, this was particularly distressing for Veronica and she vowed to shut her family out of her life. She knew that this decision violated many of her Christian principles, but she found it hard to love, impossible to forgive and easy to nurture hatred. She knew that her relationships were not pleasing to God, and that her attitudes were self-destructive. She found it very difficult to frame the question to ask God where she should be. But she was sure that her spirit was in the wrong place. She was at a crossroads.

Emily had great career prospects in information technology. Her company had a number of major international clients and she travelled extensively. She was thirty years old when she married *Howard*. They met while attending a seekers course where they both committed their lives to Christ and became enthusiastic young Christians. They quickly started asking if they were where God wanted them to be. A year or two into their marriage, they became anxious about how little they were seeing each other. Work demands and travel schedules made quality time together virtually impossible, and they knew of many young professionals whose marriages had failed in similar situations. Howard worked with a charity that had many overseas commitments. Emily and Howard both knew that something had to change – especially when they decided to start a family. Months before the twins were born, they had made a fairly radical decision after much prayer. Howard would leave his job and become involved part-time in a local Christian charity associated with their church. Emily would return to full-time work after her pregnancy leave. This was not easy, and there were some real stresses associated with the change in roles – not least because of how others perceived their choice. But both were clear that this was where the Lord wanted them to be, and they were content with their decision.

REFLECTION:

To walk out of God's will is to walk into nowhere. (C.S. Lewis)

Where does God want you to be?

Search for God's will

It is usually at life's crossroads experiences that we search most intensely for God's will. When we ask God if we are where he wants us to be, we are really asking him either to confirm that we are in his will or to show us how we have strayed from it. Few of us could honestly say that we have consistently applied the truth of Psalm 16:8 to our lives. Because the Lord has not "always been before" many of us, we too easily lose a sense of the power of his right hand and are shaken. Such is the deadening effect of sin that at times we do not even realize that we have been shaken and driven off course by other preoccupations. Bernard Edinger reminds us that "Inside the will of God there is no failure. Outside the will of God there is no success." As we saw in Chapter 4, we are easily deceived and deluded by success measures set by the world around us.

Each one of us needs to work with (rather than against) the Lord to accomplish his plans through us. This requires us first to affirm that such plans exist, and second to expect to be called to implement them. "But the plans of the LORD stand firm for ever, the purposes of his heart through all generations."[1] The age-old Christian challenge thereafter is to be continuously open to the many different ways in which the Spirit of God reveals these plans to us. The Holy Spirit called Barnabas and Saul in a vision. "Set apart for me Barnabas and Saul for the work to which I have called them".[2] When Jesus was sending out the 12 disciples he gave them a practical promise. "At that time you will be given what to say, for it will not be you speaking, but the Spirit of your Father speaking through you."[3] The Spirit also speaks to us through the Bible – the book that records the voice of God as holy men and women heard it. We would do well to remember this about the Bible: "For the word of God is living and active. Sharper than any double-edged sword, it penetrates even to dividing soul and spirit, joints and marrow; it judges the thoughts and attitudes of the heart."[4] We can learn about God's will for our lives through reading this word, hearing it preached and meditating on it. As Peter said, "For prophecy never had its origin in the will of man, but men spoke from God as they were carried along by the Holy Spirit."[5] Jesus himself gave us an insight into the unique spiritual experience that is involved in reading the Bible: "The words I have spoken to you are spirit and they are life."[6] The Holy Spirit is also an inner witness in the hearts of Christians, giving us guidance about being in the right place and doing the right thing. "The Spirit himself testifies with our spirit that we are God's children."[7] God designed us to have this relationship with him, as a father and his children converse about the daily things of life. If we are continually puzzling about God's will, we probably need to check the foundations of our relationship with him. For as Jesus promised, "But when he, the Spirit of truth, comes, he will guide you into all truth. He will not speak on his own; he will speak only what he hears, and he will tell you what is yet to come."[8]

REFLECTION:

As you reflect on your search for God's will, prayerfully answer the following questions:

Do I recognize God's authority in the Bible?

Is my reading of the Bible a "spiritual experience" or a ritual?

Has God given me answers that I have chosen to ignore? If so, what are they?

How have I responded to the voice of the Spirit?

George Macdonald said, "I find doing the will of God leaves me no time for disputing about his plans." Although this is true, it is not always easy. Jesus pleaded with his Father in Gethsemane that the cup would pass from him, and Paul earnestly prayed that the "thorn in his flesh" would be removed. Neither of these desires was realized, although both Jesus and Paul were where God wanted them to be. It can seem as though God meets our requests with silence, but even in his silence he is telling us something.[9] Not only is this not easy, but it takes more time than we want to devote to it – and so it also displaces other things. Firstly, we do need to devote time to it. And, secondly, we need to learn that God's time schedule and ours may not be well synchronized. But the consequences are such that we need to devote ourselves to seeking and obeying God's will. For, in the sobering words of C.S. Lewis, "There are only two kinds of people in the end: those who say to God, 'Thy will be done', and those to whom God says in the end, 'Thy will be done.'"[10]

People in the right place

It can be very helpful to look at the struggles and trials of the Bible's heroes and heroines. Real people in the throes of real life leap out of its pages. Not all of them started where God wanted them to be. Some required years of preparation for their role, others were stubbornly resistant to God's plans. Some had to be brought to several different crossroads before and during the time they were following God's will for them. Following are incidents from the lives of some of these characters from whom we can learn.

Philip – in a desert: God gave Philip detailed instructions about where he wanted him to go. "Go south to the road – the desert road – that goes down from Jerusalem to Gaza."[11] Here we have a classic case of Spirit-led evangelism. This was a remarkable opportunity and a strategic move for the mission of the church. Philip needed this assurance of his call before he approached the man of distinction he was to meet along the way. He may not have known the exact purpose of his journey into the desert. As Philip was being prepared, so was the Ethiopian treasurer. It's possible that he followed Jewish teaching, and probable that he was reading Isaiah from a Greek scroll. What is certain is that he had a hungry soul. While in his professional life he had authority, honour and responsibility, he recognized a gap in his knowledge – namely that he did not understand what he was studying. So we read, "Then Philip began with that very passage of Scripture and told him the good news about Jesus."[12] Philip was equipped to do this – he was in the right place, with the right knowledge and the right spirit. In order for us to be effective witnesses, the Lord usually needs us to "be in the right place" in more than one dimension of our lives. Philip knew the power of the gospel and believed in it. He would have agreed with Augustine, who said that "If you believe what you like in the gospel, and reject what you don't like, it is not the gospel you believe, but yourself." The Ethiopian believed and was baptized and Philip's mission moved on. You might well wish that your affirmation from God was equally simple and direct. Before you come to the conclusion that it was not, however, retrace your steps to make sure that you have not ignored an equally simple direction to cross your street, go to the other side of town, or to the next floor in your office block with the gospel message.

Moses – on a mountain: When Moses came down from the mountain with the tablets in his hands, "he was not aware that his face was radiant because he had spoken with the LORD".[13] Moses did not always have a shining face, nor were his attitudes always pleasing to God. At different times in his life he resisted God's call to leadership, ignored his instructions and frequently found the task of leading his people to be well nigh impossible. On this occasion, his radiance was preceded by a fresh encounter with God over a 40-day period. Such a manifestation of their leader's covenant relationship with God was essential for the Israelites to see – it changed his face, and much else besides. Do our lives shine for Christ? Are we radiant from our encounter with God? We are unlikely to be so if we are not where God wants us to be. Paul's teaching links us to this event in Moses' life. "And we, who with unveiled faces all reflect God's glory, are being transformed into his likeness with ever-increasing glory, which comes from the Lord, who is the Spirit."[14] What evidence do we show of having been with Jesus? At times we show very little. Alistair Begg once said, "If you can't shine, you can at least twinkle." Moses' experience reminds us what we need to do to have a shining face. We have to be men and women of God – and that we can't fake; we need time in God's presence – a meal, not a snack; we must be willing to climb the mountain – we cannot be content in the foothills; and we have to have a sense of mission for our lives – not treating it as a set of random walks.

Jeremiah – in the firing line: Not for the first time, Jeremiah was given an awesome challenge. Part of his mandate was to tell the nation on God's behalf to "Obey me and do everything I command you, and you will be my people, and I will be your God."[15] While God's instruction to the prophet was clear, the people were either indifferent or hostile. Jeremiah clearly felt great pressure, even though he was where God wanted him to be. Nobody was prepared to listen; the people had as many gods as they had towns; their minds were on other things; God had told him not to pray for the nation because he would not listen; and his own life was under threat. Apart from that, Jeremiah's job was easy! Perhaps it's not surprising that Jeremiah complained about where God had put him. He asked for explanations. "Why does the way of the wicked prosper? Why do all the faithless live at ease?"[16] And he wondered about the impossibility of his task in a nation of people who named God, but whose hearts were far from him. God gave him answers. He said that he could never do this job himself, that he too was suffering pain from the nation's disobedience, and that his sovereignty remained intact. Jeremiah, in short, persevered so that God's purposes would be fulfilled. You may well have parallel experiences – where your mission and location are clear, but where the going is really tough. Erwin Lutzer reminds us where our strength and focus is to be in these situations. "God often puts us in situations that are too much for us so that we will learn that no situation is too much for him."

Dorcas – in the community: Dorcas is famous for her garment-making skills. We know nothing about her background, but we know a little about her work and the impact that her life had on the community at Joppa. Luke characterizes her as "always doing good and helping the poor".[17] Her charitable activity suggests that she was a Christian with some degree of affluence. And while her name means "gazelle" – an emblem of beauty – we know less about her physical appearance than we do about the beauty of her life. In addition to other philanthropic ministries, she made robes and other clothing for local widows. Her apparently sudden death caused great grief in her community – not least among those she supported. Knowing that Peter had displayed supernatural powers and that he was in the area, he was immediately sent for. Peter came and raised her from the dead – to the astonishment and delight of both the church and the needy in the community. The miracle of her resurrection had a profound effect as the news spread like wildfire throughout the city. Luke reports that many people believed in the Lord as a result. Peter stayed on in Joppa, doubtless to build up the church with these many new converts. The story of Dorcas teaches us many lessons. Her aspirations were to be at home in service rather than have a leadership role; she was highly respected for what she did inside and outside of church circles; and God used her in both her life and death. In short, she was where God wanted her to be, using her resources and skills for him. Can we say the same of our lives?

Martha – in the home: Based on the incident in their Bethany home, Martha sometimes gets a bad press when compared to her sister Mary.[18] It's too simplistic, however, to see Martha as active and impulsive and Mary as spiritual and reflective. Martha's home was a place of good order and fine hospitality. Jesus apparently regularly visited there, resting from his intense schedule. Martha was clearly interested in his teaching, and both she and her sister sat at Jesus' feet. For Martha (and doubtless for Mary), it was not a matter of either hospitality or listening – it was both. Yet, in her distraction and anxiety concerning her on-going tasks, she did complain. "Lord, don't you care that my sister has left me to do the work by myself? Tell her to help me!"[19] While Martha's rebuke was directed to both Mary and Jesus, Jesus' response did not condemn her activity or her practical concerns for her household. The reproof is affectionate and understanding and reflects some sadness and surprise at her outburst. Was she where the Lord wanted her to be at that moment in time? In terms of her overall role in life, undoubtedly she was – but in terms of her attitude, probably not. Jesus loved both of these sisters, in spite of their different personalities and temperaments. Serving and learning are both critical parts of our character formation as disciples. Those of us with personalities like Martha's – and there are many of us – would do well to remember these words from Oswald Chambers: "Worry is an indication that we think that God cannot look after us."

Journey to Nineveh

The question of whether we are where God wants us to be will bring Jonah to mind – that reluctant prophet who rejected God's directions to go to Nineveh. Before we settle into a comfortable and complacent critique of this man, we need to think about J.I. Packer's wise words. "The church . . . is a hospital in which nobody is completely well, and anyone can relapse at any time."[20] Jonah was rebellious, self-centred and self-willed as he ran away from the Lord – but so are we at times. Perhaps this is best revealed by the fact that many of us also have a Nineveh in our lives – a place where God wants us to go, but where we refuse to go. As we noted earlier in the chapter this could be anything, including a location, a relationship or a set of attitudes. Like Jonah, we may be afraid of going there. It might be a broken relationship that will be painful to mend; a God-given job opportunity which will require a radical change of lifestyle; or an opportunity to witness that we think carries too high a risk of rejection. But Jonah got a second chance to be obedient. And

the process by which this occurred offers us a model for prayer when we, too, are disobedient, in a dark place and in deep trouble. First, Jonah was honest with God about where he was and how he got there. "In my distress I called to the LORD, and he answered me. From the depths of the grave I called for help".[21] Like Jonah, we need to own our own problem. It's an essential milestone on the journey to recovery. Second, Jonah was willing to change and pledged himself to God. "When my life was ebbing away, I remembered you, LORD, and my prayer rose to you, to your holy temple . . . But I, with a song of thanksgiving, will sacrifice to you. What I have vowed I will make good."[22] Third, Jonah was prepared to trust God with the outcome. It was only when Jonah gave his life to God that God gave it back to him. A restored Jonah then went to Nineveh, his simple message was willingly received and the whole town turned to God. Jonah's reaction is astounding. He was intensely angry because God did not do what he wanted – namely put everybody in the city to death. Having vented his anger against God, he climbed a hill outside the city and sulked. We probably all know Christians today who, when God's work does not go as they had planned, simply walk off the job. As Jonah shelters under a wilting vine God gives him a lesson on priorities – he seemed to care more about the vine than the rescued people of the city. So, after such a struggle, Jonah ends in the right place with the wrong attitude. Isn't it good that God is patient?

SELAH:

A little faith will bring your soul to heaven, but a lot of faith will bring heaven to your soul. (D.L. Moody)

Do you have a "Nineveh" where the Lord wants you to go? If so, have you tried to use Jonah's model of prayer to prepare for the journey?

With which of the five Bible characters above did you most identify? What can you learn from his or her situation that will help you to understand where the right place is for you?

1 Ps. 33:11.
2 Acts 13:2.
3 Mt. 10:19,20.
4 Heb. 4:12.
5 2 Pet. 1:21.
6 Jn. 6:63.
7 Rom. 8:16.
8 Jn. 16:13.
9 For a further exploration of this important issue see Philip Yancey, *Seeing in the Dark* (London: Marshall, Morgan & Scott, 1989).
10 For a challenging look at submitting to God's will see Rebecca Manley Pippert, *A Heart for God* (Carlisle: Authentic Lifestyle, 2003), esp. ch. 8.
11 Acts 8:26.
12 Acts 8:35.
13 Ex. 34:29.
14 2 Cor. 3:18.
15 Jer. 11:4.
16 Jer. 12:1.
17 Acts 9:36.
18 Lk. 10:38–42.
19 Lk. 10:40b.
20 J.I. Packer, *A Quest for Godliness* (Wheaton, IL: Crossway Books, 1990), 22.
21 Jon. 2:1.
22 Jon. 2:7,9.

10

Aim to Honour God in All Things

"May the words of my mouth and the meditation of my heart be pleasing in your sight, O LORD, my Rock and my Redeemer." (Ps. 19:14)

Outline

In everything that we have considered throughout this book, there is no higher aim for the Christian than to honour God.

What does honouring God involve?: Honouring God requires worship, sacrifice, energy and obedience.

The choice to honour or dishonour: How is it that many find themselves on the slippery slope that leads to dishonour? How can we learn from the tragic mistakes of others?

Honour God in the detail: What is the biblical instruction on the specifics of God-honouring lives?

What does honouring God involve?

In light of all that we have considered throughout this book, we understand that all Christians need to answer some fundamental and unavoidable questions. What do you regard as the ultimate aim of your life? How does that aim differ from those aims you are pursuing in the normal routines of life? Are the two compatible? If not, what are you planning to do about it? The Bible spells out the answer to the first of these questions with great clarity. You would find it difficult to miss this answer, in fact – unless, of course, that was your intention. One of the references, for example, is this: "Ascribe to the LORD the glory due to his name; worship the LORD in the splendour of his holiness."[1] In order to begin to address how we honour God in all things, we need to bring the lofty heights of that majestic call to worship into the office, college, home, church or workplace in which we practice our Christianity. The following is one of many verses that help us to take that transition. These are Paul's words put into contemporary language. "So here's what I want you to do, God helping you: Take your everyday, ordinary life – your sleeping, eating, going-to-work and walking-around life – and place it before God as an offering."[2] This takes us straight to the heart of the matter. Honouring God involves much more than holding him in high regard, respecting or esteeming him, being reverential in his presence and so on. While all of these attitudes are necessary, they are never sufficient. Honouring God involves nothing less than worshipping him with our heart, soul and lives. To do that, we first have to know who he is – which is why we need to study the Bible. J.I. Packer laments that "The spirit of our modern age spawns great thoughts of man and leaves room for only very small thoughts of God." Perhaps that is why so few of us effectively honour God in our lives.

We need to dig deeper to understand our motivation for honouring God. The root of the word that the New Testament regularly uses for honour is associated with the concept of "value". We can, for example, see the practical application of this idea related to sexual morality in this next verse that brings honouring God into an important area of human behaviour. "You are not your own; you were bought at a price. Therefore honour God with your body."[3] Passages such as the following develop this thought and apply it to all aspects of our lives. "If anyone purifies himself from what is ignoble, then he will be a vessel for noble use, consecrated and useful to the master of the house, ready for any good work."[4] These texts, and many others like them, teach us that honouring God requires both obedience and energy. We also need to make God-advised choices with our lives – choices that affect all aspects of our attitudes and behaviour. But there's more. Identifying with God and bearing the title "Christian" have further implications that take us back to the third commandment. "You shall not misuse the name of the LORD your God, for the LORD will not hold anyone guiltless who misuses his name."[5] While this commandment does prohibit swearing, profanity and false witness, its implications go much deeper. The language used in this commandment describes an attitude to God that is indifferent, irreverent and casual. It refers to speech as well as to conduct that dishonours God, including hypocrisy. This commandment explicitly condemns all behaviour that contradicts our profession of faith in Christ. Jesus addresses this issue directly: "Not everyone who says to me, 'Lord, Lord,' will enter the kingdom of heaven, but only he who does the will of my Father who is in heaven."[6] Hypocrisy is one of the principal ways that Christians dishonour God's name – by claiming certain standards and then not following them. In that sense we are in the "shop windows" of life every day, open to scrutiny and inspection. For good or ill, we are advertisements for the Christian faith. We can only pray that those who watch us have a different perspective on Christianity than the nineteenth-century atheist Friedrich Nietzsche had from observing Christians in his time: "You will have to look more redeemed if I am to believe in your Redeemer."

REFLECTION:

This list drawn up by A.W. Tozer fleshes out what true spirituality, that leads us to honour God, looks like. A person who lives out this true spirituality will have:

- the desire to be holy rather than happy
- the desire to see the honour of God advanced through our lives
- the desire to carry his cross
- the desire to see everything from God's viewpoint
- the desire to die right rather than live wrong
- the desire to see others advance at our expense
- the desire to make eternity-judgements instead of time-judgements

How do these desires feature in your life? Are they strong or weak, passive or active?

The choice to honour or dishonour

Christians are to honour God because of who he is and because we were created to honour him. C.S. Lewis said that God is the fuel that the human engine was designed to run on. Psalm 19:14 wonderfully illustrates the deepest yearning of the heart in tune with God – that we would please God and bring him honour. Honouring God starts with the heart – the very seat of our character, the centre of our spiritual life, our control tower. If we lose focus there, we lose everything. This central truth is readily captured in this proverb. "Trust in the LORD with all your heart and lean not on your own understanding; in all your ways acknowledge him, and he will make your paths straight."[7] Once we start being selective about the areas of our life in which we acknowledge him, self-sufficient in our interpretation of right behaviour or confident that we can make our own plans, it is usually not long before we start dishonouring God – often with disastrous consequences.

Few Christians purposely set out to dishonour God, yet he is regularly dishonoured, almost by default. On the way to bringing him dishonour, people have made a number of choices – whether or not they are even conscious of these decisions. Examples abound in most Christian communities. Often the situation results from an individual choosing to resolve one of life's crossroads experiences in a particular way. At times it is because someone has entered into a personal or business relationship that does not honour God. Sometimes people take opposing positions in a bitter family or church dispute that destroys any evidence of God's love for a generation or more. Others are consumed by greed, and their boundless ambition destroys both morality and integrity. Still others talk glibly of their love for God when it is evident to everyone else that they love money a great deal more. And then there are "multiple personality" Christians who play different parts depending on the stage on which they are performing. Such people are usually blind and self-centred enough to think that nobody notices their hypocrisy, but their actions bring the name of God into disrepute. And they have forgotten that God sees everything. The common thread in most of these situations is the emergence and ultimate dominance of God-substitutes in the lives of Christian disciples. As John Burroughs says, "Man is, and always has been, a maker of gods. It has been the most serious and significant occupation of his sojourn in the world." We need look no further than into our own hearts to know just how true that is.

While dishonouring God has a common root, we can see its rotten fruit in many different situations. Sadly I have seen many such situations, and you probably have as well. The following four people all professed faith in Christ but, in some way or another, and at a critical point in their lives, they failed to implement the Lord's instruction. Jeremiah saw this rejection of God time and again. "God's Message yet again: 'Go stand at the crossroads and look around. Ask for directions to the old road, the tried and true road. Then take it. Discover the right route for your souls.' But they said, 'Nothing doing. We aren't going that way.'"[8] These people knew the right way, but they took the wrong turning anyway.

Russell had grown his family transport business with great entrepreneurial skill. Previous generations had given him a sound foundation on which to build, but his ideas, energy and flair grew the business and took it on to another highly profitable level. He was a Christian, married, and had two teenage girls. With vastly increased wealth came a grand house, fast cars and even faster women. He now decided to sample everything that he claimed had been suppressed by his upbringing. For him it was a clear and conscious decision and, mysteriously, he thought that he could continue to live in a Christian disguise. He succeeded in deceiving his wife and many of his friends for many months – until he asked two of them to share in his new-found "freedom". They were stunned by the life he was leading, by his deception and the lies he was telling. His wife soon found out about his affairs and what the "business trips" really involved. His girls were devastated and haven't been in a church since. Public scandal, family crisis, separation and divorce followed. The business continued to prosper, but his life and testimony were in tatters – and God was dishonoured by his hypocrisy.

Mark had become a financial adviser and investor. His years as a professional accountant had taught him that there were easier ways to make much more money – but that not all of them were legitimate. One attractive alternative was building and developing property. The risks were high, but the rewards great. He would not have described his motivation for changing his career path as greed – but everyone else saw it clearly as they listened to him talk and watched his behaviour change. The trouble was that projects were often delayed, and some needed much more capital than either he had or could obtain by legal means. He started to engage in several God-dishonouring practices – quickly, but subtly. He did not tell his bank about the true state of his finances, the unpaid taxes, the cost overruns on his projects, the legal disputes that were delaying payments and so on. Through it all he displayed an ill-founded confidence in his own abilities and succeeded in deceiving everyone, including himself. He desperately needed cash and was able to extract large sums from vulnerable people with the promise of guaranteed, excellent returns. A downward spiral soon developed. In addition to being sanctioned for professional misconduct, he also faced serious criminal charges which resulted in a prison sentence. Pride, greed and self-deception were some of the ingredients of his downfall, and God was further dishonoured by his protestations of innocence and injustice. "I could have sorted this all out if only I had had time" he told a disbelieving friend.

William was a gifted church leader and a man of considerable professional standing. He was used to being respected in his community and rather liked being regarded as the hero. Of course, he never admitted this to anyone. But his dogmatic attitude was such that he tolerated no views contrary to his own about anything – from the choice of songbooks to the arrangements for car parking at the church. But he really specialized in "truth" – namely his interpretation of the Bible. He preached a lot about love and grace – but he didn't show much of either to anyone. By a process of self-selection all those who disagreed with him left the church, but others of like mind joined in equal numbers. The church became a replica of all that William believed – until Stephen joined. William initially welcomed Stephen and regarded him as a man of great spirituality and moral integrity – until he wanted the church to adopt a more modern translation of the Bible. William was shocked and described this as evidence of "a wolf in sheep's clothing" having entered the camp. With astonishing speed and within three months of Stephen's arrival, the church was polarized into two hostile camps. Many differences in doctrine and practice emerged as issues of contention, and both of these men displayed a mixture of stubbornness and childishness that astonished everyone. A church member passed the story of in-fighting on to a news reporter, who ran stories for weeks in the local newspaper. "Fight the good fight" and "Round 4 at the chapel" were among the headlines from the sub-editor. Stephen left the church, as did half of the congregation. William's church building is now a warehouse. With time it has become apparent that most of those involved in this church have become spiritual casualties – disappointed, disillusioned and disheartened. Years later God continues to be dishonoured in the locality as a result of this non-Christian behaviour "in his name". And people have long memories.

Richard was in his early twenties. Although he grew up in a Christian family, his parents were both busy with their careers and had taken little interest in his upbringing. Richard had no enthusiasm for school, but he had talent – a quick wit, a personable nature and an ability to influence people. He performed quite well in various sales jobs, although he changed employers with great frequency – for reasons that were not entirely obvious. He was popular and influential among his peers and exerted a lot of influence over their behaviour – including in the church context. His church leaders noticed this and prayed that he would be an influence for good. For several years he was a good influence – until he got bored and fell into bad company. This coincided with him being fired from his most recent job at a furniture store – having been suspected of stealing money. He was incensed by the way he had been treated and spoke with his church leaders about how he might regain his reputation. Over several weeks he assured them that he was innocent of all such charges, that he had been falsely accused and that nothing like this had ever happened before. Richard was always very plausible in such situations, and he charmed his leaders into believing his story. Tears regularly flowed from his eyes during these discussions, and his theatrical skills were well honed. Then came a bolt from the sky! Following a news story mentioning his name, it emerged that he faced dozens of other serious charges relating to credit card fraud in many parts of the country. Where did he go wrong? Probably at the crossroads when he decided that using his cunning was preferable to the drudgery of normal employment; and that much more money was needed to sustain the lifestyle for which he yearned than he could ever earn by honest means. Among the many tragic consequences of his downfall were the young Christians who liked William and saw him as a rather roguish role model – but who (under his influence) would not believe his accusers. Not only did William dishonour God by his conduct, but he also caused many others to do the same as they continued to follow him into the spiritual wilderness.

REFLECTION:

> I choose goodness – I will go without a dollar before I take a dishonest one. I will be overlooked before I will boast. I will confess before I will accuse. I choose goodness. (Max Lucado)

Put your life under God's microscope to see if there are ways in which you are dishonouring him. We need the Holy Spirit to help us in this difficult, self-revealing exercise. Once you have done this, ask yourself whether your lifestyle, behaviour and choices lead others to honour God. Or are you influencing others in a way that leads them to dishonour God?

Honour God in the detail

From its earliest pages the Bible establishes a vitally important principle. Not only do we honour God because of who he is, but we also honour him because of what he has done – and especially for our redemption. Rescue and worship go hand in hand. The children of Israel brought their firstfruits to God because he had delivered them from bondage in Egypt. "He [the Lord] brought us to this place and gave us this land, a land flowing with milk and honey; and now I bring the firstfruits of the soil that you, O LORD, have given me."[9] And so we, too, are asked to devote the best, the "firstfruits", of our life, energies, talents and resources to honouring God. Honouring God's name before others is simply the best way we can serve our all-sufficient God. "So whether you eat or drink or whatever you do, do it all for the glory of God."[10] But does he get the best? Or just the rest? Do we give God the leftovers when every other demand has been met? Sometimes we try to "negotiate" with God about what we plan to offer him. More often, perhaps, we pay too little attention to the quality of our offering. This can have wide-ranging consequences – some minor and easy to correct, some major and more difficult to remedy. Jeb Magruder, in an earthly court before a judge as he faced up to his misdemeanours, said the following: "I know what I have done, and your Honour knows what I have done. Somewhere between my ambition and my ideals, I lost my ethical compass." If you have realized that you are currently dishonouring God, try describing to the Lord where you stand today, using this confession as a prayer of repentance.

Honouring God means that we need to pay attention to detail as to how we live our lives. There are many biblical examples of this, the best of which exemplify the great truth of this proverb: "He who pursues righteousness and love finds life, prosperity and honour."[11] Moses, for instance, had to wait many years before his period of "active service" came along. But during these preparatory years he accepted mistreatment along with the people of God, rather than live in the palace as the son of Pharaoh's daughter. "He regarded disgrace for the sake of Christ as of greater value than the treasures of Egypt, because he was looking ahead to his reward."[12] Moses came to a crossroads and exercised a choice that brought honour both to God and to his people. He also made judgements on values and priorities that honoured God.

Daniel also had a striking faith that honoured God. In a time of much vagueness, superstition and idolatry, he was crystal clear about the God he worshipped. What he believed was not popular or politically correct in his time. Yet he did not compromise when that would have been the easy option, and God honoured him for his stand. Daniel knew the power of the God he praised. "Praise be to the name of God for ever and ever; wisdom and power are his. He changes times and seasons; he sets up kings and deposes them."[13] There are many parallels between Daniel's environment and our own – and we worship the same God.

Uzziah, King of Judah, gives us another type of example. His was a reign of two halves – good beginnings, when he listened to the word of God, and a bad ending because he then ignored God.

He achieved much in domestic affairs, battles and civil reconstruction, and his early work honoured God. The following verse summarizes these years well: "As long as he sought the LORD, God gave him success."[14] But then pride took over and he united the priestly and regal functions, abused holy places and openly challenged God. Uzziah had become so accustomed to God's help and blessing, for over twenty years, that he forgot who was really responsible for his success. Misuse of power and corruption soon followed. As he entered the temple, the priests described his downfall as they said to him, "Leave the sanctuary, for you have been unfaithful; and you will not be honoured by the LORD God."[15] Pride and dishonouring God were cause and effect in Uzziah's case. Napoleon once said, "I am not an ordinary man, and the laws of mortals and custom were never made for me." How vigilant we need to be to guard against that spirit of pride.

The Bible also gives us specific guidance on the type of Christian behaviour that brings honour to God. Much of this involves how we are to treat others. In the workplace, servants are to honour their masters; in the family, children are to honour their parents; citizens are to honour their civilian leaders; and in the church, the community is to honour their spiritual fathers. The biblical principles of financial stewardship require us to honour God with the money and possessions that we handle on his behalf. But God-honouring stewardship goes way beyond even that. As Milo Kauffman reminds us, "God gives man life, body, mind, abilities, time and possessions. He gives us the Word, redemption and the Holy Spirit. He holds man accountable for the proper use of these gifts." If we are truly honest, we frequently fail to use God's resources for God's glory.

But let's end with two encouraging examples. They both concern the blessing that flows from honouring God. The first is the story of Jabez, whose name means "pain" or "child of sorrow". This name, a reflection of how his parents saw his character and destiny, did not give him the best start in life. You can just imagine how he fared with that name among his childhood playmates. Had God not intervened, he probably would have experienced sorrow and failure throughout his life.

We know, however, that God hears the despised and elevates the lowly. As the psalmist tells us, "For he has not despised or disdained the suffering of the afflicted one; he has not hidden his face from him but has listened to his cry for help."[16] We also know that Jabez honoured God, hence these remarkable words. "Jabez was more honourable than his brothers. His mother had named him Jabez, saying, 'I gave birth to him in pain.' Jabez cried out to the God of Israel, 'Oh, that you would bless me and enlarge my territory! Let your hand be with me, and keep me from harm so that I will be free from pain.' And God granted his request."[17] Here is an amazing example of God's goodness to the broken-hearted who put him first.

The second example of encouragement comes from the Lord's prophetic words delivered through the mouth of Samuel. They were spoken to Eli's wicked sons. "Those who honour me I will honour, but those who despise me will be disdained."[18] Here the word for honour carries the sense of "making heavy" and the word for disdain the opposite meaning, "making light". God adds things to those who honour him. The blessings come in many forms, all of them for our good. All together, God's blessings are the sum of who we are as Christians and what the world around sees in us that it desires to have and can get no other way. It's not for sale in the hypermarket or on the web, we can't win it or fight for it. God alone gives his blessing to those who honour him. Honouring God requires a right relationship with him, a quietness of spirit, a life of faith and a commitment to his words and to prayer. The Christian life has to be God-honouring or it is a sham. The prophetic words that Samuel spoke contain both a promise and a warning for all Christians everywhere.

These lines from William Cowper's eighteenth-century poem *The Task* point us to the state of mind and heart in which we will best honour God.

A life all turbulence and noise may seem
To him that leads it, wise and to be praised,
But wisdom is a pearl with most success
Sought in still waters

SELAH:

The glory of God, and, as our only means to glorifying him, the salvation of souls, is the real business of life. (C.S. Lewis)

How will you put into practice what you have learned about honouring God?

One day there came along that silent shore,
While I my net was casting on the sea,
A Man who spoke as never man before,
I followed him: new life began in me.
Mine was the boat, but his the voice,
And his the call, yet mine the choice.
(George Macdonald)

---

[1] Ps. 29:2.
[2] Rom. 12:1 (*The Message*).
[3] 1 Cor. 6:19,20.
[4] 2 Tim. 2:21 (RSV).
[5] Ex. 20:7.
[6] Mt. 7:21.
[7] Prov. 3:5,6.
[8] Jer. 6:16 (*The Message*).
[9] Deut. 26:9,10.
[10] 1 Cor. 10:31.
[11] Prov. 21:21.
[12] Heb. 11:26.
[13] Dan. 2:20,21.
[14] 2 Chr. 26:5b.
[15] 2 Chr. 26:18c.
[16] Ps. 22:24.
[17] 1 Chr. 4:9,10.
[18] 1 Sam. 2:30.

11

Epilogue:
A Personal Crossroads

"But you, O God, do see trouble and grief; you
consider it to take it in hand. The victim commits
himself to you; you are the helper of the
fatherless." (Ps. 10:14)

Context

I planned this book and chose the title in the early weeks of
2004 – little realizing that I was about to face a major personal
crossroads with my health. In March 2004 I was diagnosed with
a serious recurrence of colon cancer, a disease for which I had
undergone surgery on two previous occasions over the past nine
years. The prognosis from my oncologist was poor, and my life
expectancy very limited. Both chemotherapy and radiotherapy
treatment were required urgently. When I received this news,
the contract to write this book was on my desk. The delivery date
on it was long after the consultant's view of my life span at that
time. I prayed about it and was convinced that, if it was the
Lord's purpose that the book should be written, he would
preserve my life long enough to complete it. As a result, I wrote
this book in very unusual and rather adverse circumstances –
most of it on my laptop while in hospital, attached to a pump
delivering anti-cancer drugs into my body. These visits spanned
three days every second week for almost six months. You will
not be surprised that I praise the Lord that he has given me
health and strength to finish the book. I also praise him that

he gave me this project to focus upon during these trying months. Those who know me are aware that I am the kind of restless person who needs to be mentally active. In my case, this book was literally a God-given task – but writing it was even more challenging because of its setting. It was written on a physical and spiritual battlefield. And it could be the last book that I will write.

I confess that I have thought and prayed long and hard about whether I should make any reference to my current personal circumstances in this book. The issues that this book covers are so much bigger than I am and apply to Christian discipleship in a broad sense. So the book stands on its own without this difficult chapter – one that I have not enjoyed writing, because it involved reliving some dark and difficult days. Others finally persuaded me to write this chapter, including many readers of my books and the medical staff who treated me. They felt that it would be wrong not to share something of this crossroads experience with others. I do so, then, for God's glory. I am not a hero or a spiritual superman – just an ordinary Christian with a life-threatening health problem who both trusts and struggles. I have tried to describe my experience and the lessons drawn from it as simply and honestly as possible in the hope that they will help others who share in similar trials. Perhaps it will make some of you stop, think and re-evaluate.

Standing at the crossroads

The news was shocking and the consultant's message had an air of finality about it. Given my history, and the severe back pains that I had had for many months, it was not entirely a surprise to me that my health problems were finally traced to cancer. In fact, I initiated the hospital consultation and the scan. For my wife Anna and for the whole family, the news was devastating. While I cannot speak for the others, I can give you an insight into my own heart to tell you how I was feeling. In my weakened state of general health – having lost four stones in weight – I was fragile and emotional. These emotions ranged from deep sadness to real joy in almost equal proportions during the early months of my treatment. The sadness had several roots. The prospect of early separation from the people you love is really difficult, and I felt this for all of my family, especially Anna, and the children and grandchildren in whose lives I would no longer play a part. Added to this was a consciousness that I might be experiencing the "last" of everything in my earthly life – the last spring flowers, the last events, the last opportunities to be with family and friends, the last chance to witness to countless colleagues and so on. Then there was the sadness that stemmed from feeling that I had so much still to do in my life – or so I thought. I experienced great sadness, but no regrets. I have tried to live my life under the Lord's instructions, using his resources that he had given me to manage to good effect. This is perhaps where some of the peace started to take over.

The principal source of my joy was my faith in God, my utter dependence on him in this set of circumstances and my eternal security in Christ Jesus. I knew that I could only trust, yet I regularly prayed, "Lord, I know what you *can* do in this situation, but can you show me what I have to do?" By that I meant several things. I knew that I needed a new intensity of trust and confidence in the Lord. I wanted to make sure that I had the right spirit whatever the outcome. Also, I needed the right attitude to the treatment and its multiple side-effects. These were not easy prayers, nor were they well crafted – but they were urgent and constant. I could best describe my prayer life then as a continuous series of conversations with the Lord. I have no idea where they began or ended. This dialogue continued day and night and was a great source of joy and comfort. My Scripture reading consisted almost entirely of "grazing" in the Psalms, and I drew strength from the many passages that seemed to speak directly to my pressing needs. The verse above from Psalm 10:14 was one of them. I had not felt truly helpless many times in my life, but this was one of those times. I knew the helper of the fatherless, but I needed to commit myself to him wholly in the terms of Psalm 10:14. That only I could do. Other psalms developed that theme in my mind. "On my bed I remember you; I think of you through the watches of the night. Because you are my help, I sing in the shadow of your wings. My soul clings to you; your right hand upholds me."[1] I slept very little through these nights, but they were refreshing times of closeness with God and, curiously, I did not feel exhausted in the mornings at that time. I needed little encouragement to cling, and I did feel God's right hand upholding me. The following verse, too, was particularly precious. "Praise be to God, who has not rejected my prayer or withheld his love from me!"[2] You will have noticed that the theme texts for each chapter throughout this book are from the Psalms. This is not a coincidence. I chose them during this period, and many of them are indelibly printed on my mind. I have rarely experienced such rich times of meditation, and at times they brought indescribable surges of joy. As never before, the joy of the Lord truly was my strength.

Throughout this period I also sensed peace, knowing that I had asked the Lord where he wanted me to be for many years and had done my best to listen to him. While I could, of course, have used some of the time differently, been more obedient and managed my priorities better, I had committed my life to his service long ago. This was just as well, I thought, as there may be very little time left. Did I think of this as a crossroads? I undoubtedly did. In some ways, however, it was a one-way option – I had to go ahead with the prescribed treatment. Not only did I feel seriously unwell, such that I was open to anything that might alleviate my pain, but I also had to go ahead for the sake of my wife and family. The critical issue for me was to cling to the only person who could take me through this unknown experience. Realizing that, I found these poetic words from Annie Johnson Flint an enormous help. This was my "Red Sea" experience, and only the Lord God could see me through it. The poem exactly captured how I saw my situation.

> Have you come to the Red Sea place in your life
> Where, in spite of all you can do
> There is no way out, there is no way back
> There is no other way but through?

I knew that I was not alone – both because of the Lord and his people. It seemed only days before the news of my illness spread around the Christian community at home and abroad. As a result, we have had widespread and sustained prayer support from many different parts of the world. These prayers, along with the accompanying telephone calls, emails, letters and cards, have been wonderful and a great blessing to all of us. I called all of my business and professional colleagues to tell them personally about my illness. Their reactions on the whole consisted of several versions of "shock and horror", not least because I had been so transparent with them. All were totally supportive, some were dumbstruck, some were visibly moved, and many pointed to my faith as something that would be able to sustain me. Some told me quite openly that many people would be watching how I handled this crisis with my health – no pressure there! Some business associates told me for the first time of their Christian faith and assured me of their prayers. Later in this chapter I will discuss what we can all learn from the range of reactions that people with cancer seem to elicit from those around them.

In the early months of treatment my mind was hyperactive. There were so many things that I wanted to think through – about my illness, about the themes in this book, but most of all about what my faith really meant in times like this. With regard to the latter, one thought dominated. And it still does. The following verse has been on my study wall for many years: "My times are in your hands".[3] For a long time I implicitly accepted the truth of E.F. Hallock's remark: "That my times are in God's hand is a fact whether I realize and experience it or not." But now this issue of actively choosing to rest in God had a new sense of urgency. I knew that "my times" included every single aspect of my life and all of my circumstances – good and bad. I understood that God knew all about giving us "24–7" attention before it ever became a modern sound-bite. I thought about the fact that things that are in someone's hands are there for a purpose – for carrying, touching, working, expressing, rejoicing, writing and so on. I, too, am in God's hands for a purpose, and I was awestruck to realize that all of God is involved in keeping me in his hands. Based on this and related meditations, my constant cry has been to acknowledge, "Lord, I am in your hands – thank you. There is no other place I would rather be." I must have prayed this prayer hundreds of times over the past months. You will note how simple it is. There's no complex composition to it. It's just a cry from a heart in desperate need. Each time I prayed these words, God assured me that he is in complete control of both my life and my allotted time-span. Others may influence, but they will never control. Some will shape, but they will not determine. Thomas Fuller wisely said, "Man is immortal till his work is done." I have total assurance that this is true, and that what the Lord intends me to do will not be left undone.

What have I learned?

About God's plans: That they are unfathomable, yet perfect. Would I have chosen this path? No, certainly not. Yet these past months have been a unique combination of both trial and blessing. The source of the trial is obvious. The blessing, however, is multi-faceted. I see God's blessing in, among other things, the incredible prayer support of the Christian community, the awesome opportunities to witness to so many people, the shalom of God in my heart and a sense of being preserved once more to fulfil his purpose for me. As a result, many familiar verses have taken on new meaning. Among them is this one from Jeremiah: "'For I know the plans I have for you,' declares the LORD, 'plans to prosper you and not to harm you, plans to give you hope and a future.'"[4] It's a good thing that we don't know the plan, but we draw great strength from knowing the planner. This experience has taken my understanding of spiritual prosperity to a new level. And the many-sided, holistic peace of God is wonderful.

About myself: I have never asked why this has happened to me – although I know many others have. This question is not mine to ask if I really trust the Lord. But I confess that I did not immediately see that this experience was for God's glory. I have come to see that now, mainly through the testimony opportunities the experience has created. The truth is that none of us know how we will react in such circumstances until we are in them and different people, including Christians, come to terms with illness in different ways. I have found these thoughts from Robert Murray McCheyne to be challenging yet helpful.

> Every wise workman takes his tools away from the work from time to time that they may be ground and sharpened; so does the only-wise Jehovah take his ministers oftentimes away into darkness and loneliness and trouble, that he may sharpen and prepare them for harder work in his service.

Tough though it sounds, and feels, he is right. During these past months I have, on several occasions, had a great sense of elation about heaven. This renewed hope of heaven has helped me to put my intense interest in all that I am engaged in here into perspective – and it has reminded me that the best is yet to come.

About others: In such a situation as mine, the most important "others" are those nearest and dearest to the person with the illness. This experience has perhaps been even more difficult for them than it has been for me. They have to watch, pray, support and worry about the consequences. They need special prayer. Cancer is a very difficult illness for many people to confront. I have learned a lot from the facial expressions of people when I have told them about my illness. And this range of reactions is understandable. How others react has, in my experience, a lot to do with the attitude of the one who is ill. I felt it was essential for me to be open and positive, and to help to set my illness in context for anyone who was prepared to listen – especially non-Christians. I could not speak highly enough of the caring and prayerful attitude of the Christian community. I didn't expect people to say much when they met me – I was encouraged simply by the reminder that they were praying for me and my family. But even that is impossible for some people. Here I would give some gentle advice – "If you meet us, talk to us – however little you say." I have been surprised (and sometimes saddened) by the number of experienced and mature people I know who don't seem able to do that. I have spoken to other Christian cancer sufferers who have had the same experience. It's difficult, but it has to be overcome – particularly in a Christian environment.

About the Lord: Thomas Aquinas once said, "God is so powerful that he can direct any evil to a good end." This experience has taught me so much about the sovereignty of God and about how our individual lives fit into his plan. I have an acute sense that I need to capture in my mind all the lessons I have learned from him, and I closely relate to this verse: "Remember today what you have learned about the Lord through your experiences with him."[5] As a result, "What do I do with the time that is left?" is the most critical and recurring question I now ask. Of course, this is not a question that should only occur to us in times of duress – but at such times the question presents itself with a new clarity and fresh urgency. Rick Warren has said, "What matters is not the duration of your life, but the donation of it."[6] I was encouraged to read this observation and prayed that I would focus on continuing to give my life to God's service, regardless of the amount of time I have. In all of this, I bow to the truth of these sober words from Dietrich Bonhoeffer: "God has reserved to Himself the right to determine the end of life, because he alone knows the goal to which it is His will to lead it. It is for Him alone to justify a life or to cast it away."

About trials: I have been aware for a long time that the Christian life gives me no immunity from suffering. But now I have also experienced the Lord's smelting process doing its work. I accept (perhaps rather reluctantly) Kenneth Wuest's observation that suffering is always used by a God of love to refine our lives. "It burns out the dross, makes for humility, purifies and increases our faith, and enriches our lives."[7] Indeed it does just that – and in the process perspectives and priorities change, faith becomes everything, values are reassessed, vision is clarified, the Lord becomes more precious, and reality emerges through the mist and noise of life. Moreover, I now take another form of comfort from these encouraging words from Peter. "Friends, when life gets really difficult, don't jump to the conclusion that God isn't on the job. Instead, be glad that you are in the very thick of what Christ experienced. This is a spiritual refining process, with glory just around the corner."[8] I thank the Lord that he is always "on the job". Although trials are designed to have a positive impact on our faith, this is not always the case. The following verse helps me a lot in this respect, especially put in these words: "What is faith? It is the confident assurance that what we hope for is going to happen. It is the evidence of things we cannot yet see."[9]

Final remarks

As I complete this book, I am in much better health. My treatment is over and the consultants have variously described my response to it as "remarkable" and "spectacular". I have had several interesting conversations with my oncologist about this. He naturally claims that the mix of drugs selected has been optimal for attacking the disease. I give him full credit for that, but I also remind him that there are several other key variables at work over which he has no control. These include the sovereignty of God who sets the times for men, the prayers of many hundreds of his people and the spirit that the Lord gave me. In these matters, I am content to leave the attribution to the Lord. You might have guessed that C.S. Lewis is one of my favourite writers. I have returned time and again to these words from his pen: "God, who foresaw your tribulation, has specially armed you to go through it, not without pain but without stain." I pray that that would be so.

From my many years of writing, this book stands out because of the testing circumstances in which I wrote it. Among other things, these circumstances have influenced its content, its underlying passion and its call for urgent responses. I pray that this book will help each of its readers in some way to further unlock the potential for God that exists within all of our lives. This can only happen by the power of the Spirit, since he enables us to discover the joy of obedience and our spiritual prosperity. These crossroads experiences inevitably reflect my own journey. I hope and pray that this book will enhance and enrich yours. The most important consideration in all of this is to allow Jesus to be the "Lord of all of our crossroads". Meanwhile, we all remain in his hands.

SELAH:

These words from Isaac Watts are so rich in hope and promise. Their positive message is a fitting end to this book – for all who read it and who share in the trials of life, looking for God's purpose in them. Each day we have is full of opportunity, if only we can seize it.

> The Lord can clear the darkest skies
> Can give us day for night
> Make drops of sacred sorrow rise
> To rivers of delight.

[1] Ps. 63:6 – 8.
[2] Ps. 66:20.
[3] Ps. 31:15a.
[4] Jer. 29:11.
[5] Deut. 11:2 (TEV).
[6] Warren, *The Purpose Driven Life*, 233.
[7] Kenneth S. Wuest, *Bypaths in the Greek New Testament* (Grand Rapids: Eerdmans, 1940), 73.
[8] 1 Pet. 4:12,13 (*The Message*).
[9] Heb. 11:1 (NLT).